THE POWER OF MULTI-SENSORY PREACHING AND TEACHING

We have all heard the statistics, that listeners retain a lot more of what we are saying if we can help them to do more than simply hear it. Believing the statistics to be true, we have dabbled with object lessons, drama, and PowerPointTM, all in the effort to utilize a broader range of sensory appeal. Finally, now we have a resource that confirms what we have long suspected. Rich Blackwood not only gives us the research, but he gives us a method that is practical, sustainable, and steeped in expository conviction. This is a book for preachers that are already good at what they do, increasing their communication quotient so as to deepen their listener's engagement with the Word.

KENTON C. ANDERSON
AUTHOR OF *CHOOSING TO PREACH*, AND WWW.PREACHING.ORG
PROFESSOR OF HOMILETICS, ACTS SEMINARIES OF TRINITY WESTERN UNIVERSITY

When Jesus preached he immersed people in truth. Rick Blackwood will help you do the same.

DR. J. KENT EDWARDS
PROFESSOR OF PREACHING & LEADERSHIP
DIRECTOR, DOCTOR OF MINISTRY PROGRAM
TALBOT SCHOOL OF THEOLOGY / BIOLA UNIVERSITY

CREASE **ATTENTION, COMPREHENSION, AND RETENTION**

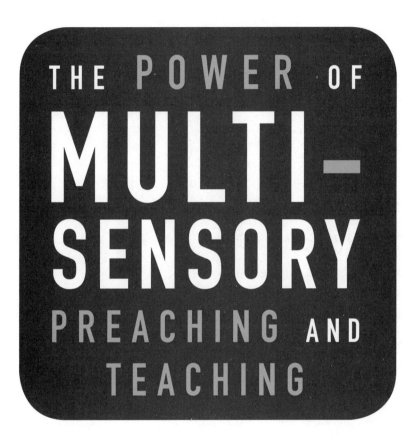

THE POWER OF

MULTI-SENSORY

PREACHING AND TEACHING

RICK BLACKWOOD

ZONDERVAN®

ZONDERVAN.com/
AUTHOR**TRACKER**
follow your favorite authors

 ZONDERVAN®

The Power of Multisensory Preaching and Teaching
Copyright © 2008 by Rick Blackwood

Requests for information should be addressed to:

Zondervan, *Grand Rapids, Michigan 49530*

Library of Congress Cataloging-in-Publication Data

Blackwood, Rick, 1956 –.
    The power of multisensory preaching and teaching : increase attention, comprehension,
and retention/ Rick Blackwood.
        p. cm.
    Includes bibliographical references.
    ISBN 978-0-310-28097-2 (hardcover jacketed)
    1. Preaching – Audio-visual aids. I. Title.
BV4227.B53 2008
268'.635 – dc22   2008016850

Interior design by Sherri L. Hoffman

Printed in the United States of America

08 09 10 11 12 13 14 • 25 24 23 22 21 20 19 18 17 16 15 14 13 12 11 10 9 8 7 6 5 4 3 2 1

To my wife Rhonda

Rhonda, I dedicate this book to you, though one page does not begin to contain the space I need to say, "thank you." I wish I could write an entire book to describe to the world the reasons why my life is happier, more peaceful, more fulfilled, and a million times more fun because of you. In the words of Stevie Wonder, "You are the sunshine of my life."

I will never forget the first time I laid eyes on you. I thought to myself, "I have never seen a girl more beautiful!" You took my breath away then, and you still take it away today. I had no idea that you would consider dating a guy like me, much less marrying me, but you did! It had to be a "God thing!"

Our journey in life has been nothing short of thrilling. From our dating days, to our days in college, to our first and second child, to the churches God has allowed us to serve, to our brand new grand-baby, it has been awesome.

Thank you for being the constant encourager in my life. There are things I never could have done or accomplished without you by my side. Writing this book is certainly one of them.

I hope I have been able to bring some of the joy to your life that you have so brought to mine. It seems appropriate to dedicate a book on *phenomenal* communication to a wife who epitomizes the word "phenomenal."

CONTENTS

ACKNOWLEDGMENTS

God has blessed my ministry by surrounding me with people who can overcome my inadequacies. That has been the case at Christ Fellowship, and it was the case in the production of this work. *The Power of Multisensory Preaching and Teaching* is the product of many minds, and the following acknowledgments are not just obligatory thanks. These are heart-felt gratitude to everyone involved.

Christ Fellowship, I want to begin with you. You are the joy and rejoicing of my heart before the Lord. The research conducted in this book was made possible because of the wonderful tapestry that God has woven together in you. I love you all from the bottom of my heart.

Brad Waggoner of the Southern Baptist Theological Seminary, thank you so much for steering me through the research and writing of my dissertation. Without your patience and guidance, I never would have made it through.

Michael Anthony of Talbot School of Theology, thank you for giving me direction in the research design of this work. I scribbled your instructions on the back of a napkin at Southern Seminary, but I often referred back to them like a guiding light.

Research Team, I thank all of you for the painstaking work you invested during the research phase of this project. Paulette Johnson and Debbie Sutton, thank you for your statistical expertise.

Eric Geiger, thank you for bringing a culture of excellence to Christ Fellowship. It has made all the difference in the life of our church.

All the staff at Christ Fellowship, thank you for making Christ Fellowship a wonderful place to work and serve. I love you all!

The Design Team and Worship Team of Christ Fellowship, thank you for making my sermons multisensory. Your creativity and talents continue to amaze me week after week after week. Thank you to Alex Fagundo for taking such wonderful photographs for this work.

Paul Engle, thank you for being my editor and believing in me throughout this process. Your wisdom and encouragement have helped me at every step of this journey. Finally, thanks to Zondervan for giving me this opportunity.

PRESENTING THE MULTISENSORY EFFECT

But solid food belongs to those who are of full age, that is,
those who by reason of use have their senses exercised to
discern both good and evil.

HEBREWS 5:14 NKJV

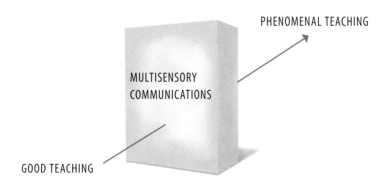

In his landmark book, *Good to Great,* Jim Collins says, "Good is the enemy of great. And that is one of the key reasons why we have so little that becomes great."[1] Collins writes that statement in the context of business organizations, but the same truth can be applied to teaching. The enemy of *great* teaching is *good* teaching.

Many pastors and Christian educators settle for good teaching when they could easily elevate to great teaching, indeed to phenomenal teaching. The goal of this work is to show you a strategy of communication that can help you make that leap.

CHAPTER 1

WELCOME:
TO THE MULTISENSORY REVOLUTION

Equipped with five senses, man explores the universe around him and calls the adventure science.

EDWIN HUBBLE

Do you consider yourself a *good* communicator or a *great* communicator? If you consider yourself a *good* communicator, would you like to elevate to *great*? If you are already a *great* communicator, would you like to raise the bar to *phenomenal*? You can! And *relax!*—it's not going to complicate your life.

Imagine teaching the Bible with such captivation that people "sit on the edge of their seats" with interest. Imagine being so understandable that people who normally "don't get it" do in fact "get it" when you teach. Imagine being so graphic and so explicit in your explanations of biblical content that people find it unforgettable. Captivating, understandable, and unforgettable. Can you imagine the effect?

Think of the effect on your church! Your audience would grasp the text you teach, catch the vision you cast, and become "doers of the Word" instead of hearers only. Such is the effect of *multisensory communication*; welcome to the revolution.

Interestingly, a host of pastor-teachers already utilize this method of teaching, and they do so because of its powerful effect! It is called *multisensory* because it interfaces with *multiple senses*. Unlike conventional preaching, which stimulates only the sense of hearing, multisensory communication stimulates multiple senses—that is, the senses of hearing, seeing, touching, and sometimes even smell and taste.

Instead of engaging only the ears of your congregation, multisensory communication enables you to engage their ears, eyes, and hands, and it brings more of the whole person into the learning process.

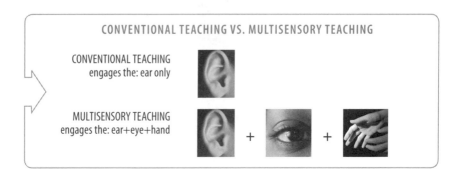

IDENTIFYING CHARACTERISTICS

The identifying characteristics of multisensory preaching are the use of props, object lessons, interactive tools, video clips, drama, art, music, thematic backdrops, food, water, smells, and other creative elements that stimulate sensory perception. A growing number of pastor-teachers are making use of multisensory communication to elevate the impact of their teaching, and they are doing so without compromising the integrity of biblical teaching.

SENSITIVE TO THE SENSES

Simply put, the multisensory teacher recognizes the senses as *information receptors*. In other words, the senses act as antennas, which receive information and then transmit that information to the brain for processing, learning, and acting.

With that neurological fact in mind, the multisensory teacher aims his teaching at as many of those receptors as possible, knowing the more senses he stimulates in the teaching, the higher the levels of learning in the audience.

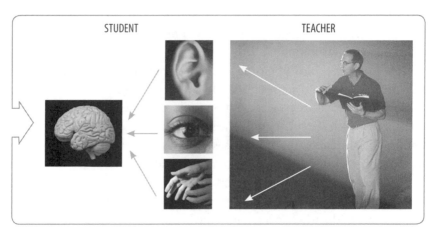

In addition, the multisensory teacher understands that people have *learning preferences* by which they *prefer* to learn and by which they learn *best*. Stated another way: Some people in our congregations prefer to learn by *hearing*; others need to *see* the concept in order to learn it; still many others learn best by *interacting* with the teacher. Bible teacher John MacArthur reminds us of *learning preferences* when he writes: "How do you learn best? Preferences vary from person to person."[1]

The multisensory communicator is sensitive to individual learning preferences and strategically plans his teaching to connect with *all* learners in his audience, not just *some* of them. Recognizing that a congregation will be filled with auditory learners, visual learners, and interactive learners, the multisensory teacher varies his teaching style and mixes verbal, visual, and interactive elements in his communication.

THE POWER OF VISUAL

During the doctoral research that gave birth to this book, I confirmed a hunch I had. People have higher levels of attention, comprehension, and retention when teaching is presented in a visually rich form. In fact, God *wired* our brains for visuals. According to 3M Corporation, we process *visuals* 60,000 times faster than *text*.[2] This is because we take in data from text in a sequential fashion, while we process visuals in an *instant*. It is said that a picture is worth a thousand words. For example, it would take at least a thousand words to tell you about how Christ Fellowship, the church in Miami where I serve, was damaged during Hurricane Andrew. Or, I could show you a picture.

Which is faster? Which is more memorable? Which etches the image into your mind?

Dr. Lynell Burmark, in her work *Visual Literacy: Learn to See, See to Learn*, says there is a natural progression in the way we process information: "First the *image*, then the *thoughts*." She tells of a letter circulating on the Internet describing a young boy's reaction to this beautiful sunset. "Dear God, I didn't *think* purple and orange went together until I *saw* the sunset you created on Tuesday. That was cool." — Eugene

"I didn't *think* until I *saw*."[3] Sometimes we don't really comprehend something until we see it. Job expressed the "seeing = comprehension" sequence when he wrote: "My ears had *heard* of you but now my eyes have *seen* you. Therefore I despise myself and repent in dust and ashes" (Job 42:5). My ears had heard, but now my eyes see. Translation? "Now that I see, I *understand* better!"

Can image-rich communication have that same effect in your congregation? Absolutely! A report published by the Xerox Corporation years ago revealed that 83 percent of what we learn comes through our sight.[4] In fact, recent research discovered that using visual imagery took 40 percent less time to explain complex ideas.[5] Helen Keller, who was mute, deaf, and blind, expressed this about sight: "Of all the senses, sight must be the most delightful."

THE POWER OF INTERACTION

During my research, I discovered another fact about which I had a hunch. People learn even more when we add interaction to verbal and visual communication. A Chinese proverb goes something like this:

> I hear, and I forget.
> I see, and I remember.
> I do, and I understand.

Though that quote may not be exact, it does highlight the effect of teaching that includes hearing, seeing, and interaction. I once heard a public school teacher talk about this approach in terms of teaching a child. She gave an example of teaching a child about the wonders of the ocean and offered three teaching options:

Option #1:   *Talk* to the child about the ocean. Now, ask the child to talk about what she learned.

Option #2:   *Talk* about the ocean and *show* the child photographs of the ocean. Show her images of its color and vast horizons. Show her pictures of the sunset. Now ask her to talk about what she has learned.

Option #3:   Go to the ocean, and insert one five-year-old. Let her *feel* the sand between her toes, let her experience the waves, let her smell the salt-water air, and let her splash and swim in the tide. Now, let's talk to her about the wonder of God's ocean.

The above sequence moves the student from a monosensory learning experience (hearing only) to a dual-sensory experience (hearing and seeing) to a multisensory experience (hearing, seeing, smelling, and touching).

The research in this book demonstrates that the more senses we stir in the learner, the higher the levels of learning. This is true in the classroom, and it is true in the worship center. Though we cannot insert our congregation into the ocean, we can insert them into the learning process. We can show them visual images and use interactive tools to involve them in the learning process. By the way, which teaching option would you prefer to learn by? 1, 2, or 3?

THE MULTISENSORY REVOLUTION

Many pastors and Christian educators have embraced the power of multisensory communication, and they have begun a preaching-teaching revolution. I use the word "revolution" because for years, traditional teaching methodologies have ignored the role of the senses in learning. All too often, traditional teaching has also ignored the different learning styles and sensory preferences through which a student maximizes learning and accelerates learning rates.

This trend has been especially pervasive in public education. Failure to recognize learning styles in public schools has promoted a standard lecture format for teaching, which has frustrated the learning of many.

Many public school educators dispatch a "one size fits all" style of teaching, i.e. lecture, and they ignore the fact that each person brings to the learning environment a unique set of learning characteristics.[6] The fact is: One "teaching style" does not fit all "learning styles."

Even more unfortunate is the fact that the church has caught "the lecture disease." The same lecture methodology that dominates public education pervades the evangelical church. As opposed to being open to the multisensory teaching models of the Bible, the church has mimicked the "one size fits all" methodology of the culture. Such lecture teaching has curtailed the full impact of teaching the Word and resulted in less "doing of the Word." It is time for a change. Educator Stephen Brookfield provokes all teachers to reflect on communication methodology when he writes:

> Sooner or later, something happens that forces the teacher to confront the possibility that they may be working with assumptions that don't really fit their situations. Recognizing the discrepancy between *what is* and what *should be* is often the beginning of the critical journey.[7]

THE MULTISENSORY REVIVAL

A "revival" of multisensory communication is taking hold in today's evangelical church. I use the term "revival," because multisensory communication is as old as the Bible itself. For years, multisensory teaching methodologies were jettisoned from the church and considered simple, unsophisticated, and even ungodly. Today, however, many pastors and Christian educators are reviving multisensory teaching strategies, and the effect is remarkable. In fact, after significant research in the disciplines of theology, neurology, and cognitive experiments, our findings conclusively demonstrate that multisensory teaching can make us more effective communicators. And if you're like this pastor, you can use all the help you can get.

All of us who teach God's Word want to captivate people's *attention*, and then impart the truth of God's Word in a way that is *understandable* and *memorable*. Multisensory communication raises that capability. It has helped many pastors and Christian teachers to be more captivating, more understandable, and more memorable.

What I love about multisensory teaching is that it transforms biblical teaching from *both* sides of the communication dynamic, that is, the teacher and the congregation.

For the teacher, multisensory communication brings the opportunity to be creative, to introduce variety, and to have outright fun in the teaching process. Oops, did I say "fun"? Multisensory teaching can keep us out of communication ruts and allow us to express ourselves from changing angles.

For the congregation, they receive a multidimensional experience. The learning process becomes more than just hearing; it becomes a hearing, visual, and participatory experience. This can make learning fun, diverse, and unforgettable.

TEACHER GIVES
— Verbal
— Visual
— Interactive
— Creativity
— Variety

AUDIENCE GAINS
— Attentiveness
— Clarity
— Memory
— Fun
— Diversity

ARE YOU INCURABLY "GOOD"?

Speaking of *good companies*, Jim Collins asks this soul-searching question: "Can a good company become a great company, and, if so, how? Or is the disease of 'just being good' incurable?"[8] Wow, that is the same question we face as communicators. Can a good communicator become a great communicator and, if so, how? Or is the disease of *just being good* incurable?

Pastors, small group leaders, and other Christian educators must communicate effectively or perish! Effective communication demands that the communicator be *captivating*, *understandable*, and *memorable*. Stated another way: Effective communicators are able to impact the cognitive domains of *attention*, *comprehension*, and *retention*.

You are not incurably "good." *The Power of Multisensory Preaching and Teaching* can help you move from *good* teaching to *great* teaching; or from *great* teaching to *phenomenal* teaching. Think about being a part of a church where you have a team of people to help you dream through the sermon communication. Imagine the joy of being creative and imaginative — most communicators are. Imagine stirring up the creative gifts of others to help you get the message across.

In Part 1, I will examine *why* multisensory communication is so powerful and *how* it can significantly elevate congregation *attention levels* as well as raising *comprehension* and *retention* status. Neurological research, theological affirmation, and cognitive experiments presented in the book conclusively demonstrate that the more senses we stimulate in our teaching, the higher the levels of audience attention, comprehension, and retention. In other words, as sensory stimulation rises in the teaching, learning levels rise in the audience.

This section also presents the marriage of biblical exposition to multisensory communication. Theological precedence is presented to demonstrate that multisensory communication and biblical exposition are not mutually exclusive.

In Part 2, you will receive practical help to prepare you to teach in a multisensory form. It also provides crucial information to prepare your congregation to receive such sermons. Finally, it provides step-by-step guidance for building a team to help you create multisensory messages.

In Part 3, this book provides practical examples for preaching and teaching in a multisensory form. Sermon examples will be presented that range from simple, to intermediate, to advanced.

Regardless of the pastor's skill level, *The Power of Multisensory Preaching and Teaching* shows the pastor *why* and *how* multisensory teaching can have people "sitting on the edge of their seats" with interest as well as learning and remembering more than ever before. As a result of reading this book, pastors, Christian educators, and even secular educators can significantly raise the bar on their communication effectiveness.

It should be noted that there are well-meaning dissenters who view this teaching style with great skepticism. Why? Because they see it only as the latest fad, which is unbiblical and compromises the dignity of biblical preaching. I understand the skepticism. *The Power of Multisensory Preaching and Teaching* counters this notion and demonstrates that this preaching style can be both *effective* and *biblical*.

Here is a list of benefits of multisensory communication:

1. Gains audience attention quicker and holds it longer
2. Brings greater clarity to teaching
3. Generates long-term retention
4. Encourages application
5. Makes teaching and learning fun (oops, I said it again)

At the end of each chapter we have included discussion questions. Take the time to grapple with these questions. Use them with your staff, small group leaders, potential creative team, and others who seek to teach the Word.

DISCUSSION QUESTIONS

1. Without looking back at the picture of the hurricane damage done to Christ Fellowship, how much of the picture can you recall in your mind's eye?

2. In terms of teaching the child about the ocean, which of the three teaching methodologies do you think would generate the greatest attention? Why?

3. If you were the child, which style of communication would you prefer to learn by? Why?

4. How would you explain the difference between monosensory and multisensory?

CHAPTER 2

ELEVATE:
FROM GOOD TO PHENOMENAL COMMUNICATION

Good is the enemy of great. And that is one of the key reasons we have so little that becomes great.

JIM COLLINS

THE DAY I CHANGED IN THE PULPIT

I couldn't believe the effect! People were literally sitting on the edge of their seat as they followed my sermon. I was taking a risk, but it was a risk I felt I had to take. Slip into the scene: I was the pastor of a large multicultural congregation in Miami, Florida, and I was about to attempt my first multisensory sermon. In my quiet time, I noticed that Jesus was a multisensory teacher. He combined verbal, visual, and interactive communication to produce this powerful effect. So, I decided to experiment with his model in the exposition of a biblical text. Here's how I prepared for the experiment.

Before the service, I set the stage area with some simple visual props. I also asked the ushers to give everyone coming into the auditorium a small instrument by which they would interact with the message. As people began entering the worship center, attention levels immediately heightened, because the stage that had looked the same for years suddenly looked different. Now there were props and visual aids atop the platform. People entered the room whispering and asking questions to one another wondering what it meant. They weren't sure what to expect.

Now it was time to see if my risk would pay off. As I began to teach using the simple visuals I had placed on the stage, I saw something that took me by surprise. People were actually leaning forward, as if on the edge of their seats with interest. They were not just *listening* to me; they were *watching* me, as if I was doing something that they just had to see.

It was patently clear that audience attention levels were elevated. Attention levels seemed to heighten even more as they interacted with the instrument that they had received. At this point, the audience seemed incapable of distraction. In fact, the only person who seemed distracted was me! I was momentarily distracted by the audience response. In the midst of my teaching, it occurred to me that they weren't merely using their ears; they were now engaging their ears, their eyes, and their hands. They were not passively engaged; they were aggressively engaged. They were not partially engaged; they appeared totally engaged — absorbed!

It was also obvious that audience comprehension levels were elevated. After the message, a number of people came up and said, "Rick, I really *understood* what you were saying, because it was so visual and interactive." A lady who was new to our church said to me, "I am a visual learner, and all the visuals helped make things crystal clear for me." Based on these anecdotal testimonies, the multisensory teaching had not only impacted attention levels, but it had also raised comprehension levels.

Then came the "aha moment." Weeks later, I noticed that people were *still* talking about that message. In fact, it was the buzz around Christ Fellowship for some time. The correlation hit me like a hammer between the eyes. My multisensory sermon had not only elevated *attention* and *comprehension* levels, but it had also increased *retention* levels. The verbal presentation combined with the power of visuals and hands-on interaction made the information stick like Velcro. The audience was able to remember what was taught in the sermon, because they heard it, saw it, and interacted with it.

LET'S DO THE MATH

Three domains of learning seemed to have been impacted by the multisensory methodology: *attention, comprehension,* and *retention.* In other words, a direct correlation appeared between the number of senses being stimulated and the levels of attention, comprehension, and retention. It seemed as if the more senses I stirred in the teaching, the more the people learned. Stated another way: As sensory levels rose, communication effectiveness seemed to rise from *good* to *great*.

Bear in mind that I had no objective data to support such a hunch. At this point, I wasn't even sure *I* believed such a correlation existed. It was difficult, however, to argue with what was happening. If "seeing is believing," then I should have been a believer in the multisensory effect. Incidentally, the message was part of a verse-by-verse expository sermon from the book of Ephesians.

DOUBLE-CHECKING THE MULTISENSORY EFFECT

After that experience, I decided to test my notion again. This time I asked one of our other pastors to teach. Tony Isaacs is our small group pastor as well as one of the teaching pastors at Christ Fellowship. As I had done in my multisensory sermon, Tony set the stage with visuals and interactive elements, and then he began to unpack his exegetical message. As the sermon unfolded, I stood behind a curtain to observe the reaction of the congregation. I was blown away by the response I witnessed.

Typically when Tony spoke, people paid attention, but this time it was remarkably different. Let me give you a visual image of what I was witnessing from behind the curtain. Lean back in your seat and imagine that you are listening to someone teach. Now, sit up and lean forward, as if some intriguing and unforgettable sight captivates you. That is what I saw as Tony was teaching. The congregation seemed so focused that nothing could have distracted them from what they were learning. They were riveted to his verbal, visual, and interactive teaching.

Tony has always been a good teacher, but he had never garnered that level of attention before. He had been transformed before my eyes from a *good communicator* to a *phenomenal communicator*.

SHOW-AND-TELL

The truth is, I had witnessed this effect years earlier in my ministry. When I was a young pastor in Charlotte, North Carolina, our small church had a children's sermon every Sunday morning in the main auditorium. This children's message was taught by a wonderful young lady who knew the multisensory effect before it was even popular. It was show-and-tell time.

Every Sunday, before I spoke to the adults, the children in the auditorium would rush to the front to be captivated by the multisensory teaching of Debbie Wendell. The children, however, weren't the only ones captivated by Debbie's teaching; the adults were also captivated — and so was the pastor! Her messages were unforgettable. To this day, they remain indelibly etched into my memory.

For example, one Sunday she was teaching about *words* that come out of our mouths. Her point was this: When we speak harmful words to someone, it is difficult to get those words back. Once they come out of our mouth, the damage they do can be difficult to undo.

To drive this point home, she gave each child a small tube of toothpaste and asked them to squeeze some out onto a piece of cardboard. Once the kids did that, she instructed them to put the toothpaste back into the tube. You can imagine the struggle they had trying to get the toothpaste back into the tube. She then drove home her lesson: Just as it is difficult to put toothpaste back into the tube once we squeeze it out, it is difficult to put words back into our mouth once they come out. Her concluding moral was simple but clear: "Be careful what comes out of your mouth."

As she finished, I thought to myself: "I am about to teach a sermon, and some of my congregation may be bored with it before I finish, but nobody was bored with Debbie's sermon!" Then I thought to myself: "I am about to teach a message that many in my congregation will forget before the day is over, but no one will forget Debbie's lesson." Why was it so powerful? It was powerful because it was verbal, visual, and interactive. The audience engaged their senses of hearing, seeing, and touching. The result was high levels of attention, comprehension, and long-term retention.

THE ANTI-BORING EFFECT

As I pondered the audience responses to Debbie's multisensory teaching, Tony's multisensory teaching, and my own multisensory teaching, something significant occurred to me. There was a common denominator in all three: no audience boredom!

The audience in all three cases appeared focused, undistracted, and totally absorbed in the teaching. In fact, there seemed to be an observable *anti-boring effect* connected to multisensory communication. I was observing that effect with my own eyes, though my question at the time was this: Is this anti-boring effect real, and if so, can it be proven?

Audience boredom is the chief enemy of all communicators. It is especially the enemy of those of us who teach God's Word, because what we teach has everlasting consequences. We cannot afford to bore our congregations, since eternal life and death are on the line. Haddon Robinson, considered one of the greatest biblical communicators of our day, warns about the deadly effects of boring our congregations:

> Boredom is like anthrax. It can kill … Dull, insipid sermons not only cause drooping eyes and nodding heads, they also destroy life and hope. What greater damage can we do to people's faith than to make them feel like God and Jesus and the Bible are as boring as the want ads in the Sunday newspaper?[1]

Whoa!

Yet, such boredom is pervasive in many churches. In the same work, Robinson goes on to give this dig to many preachers: "More people have been bored out of the faith than have been reasoned out of it."[2] Ouch!

As far back as 1857, Anthony Trollope wrote of the pain of listening to some sermons. "There is perhaps no greater hardship at present inflicted on mankind in civilized and free countries than the necessity of listening to sermons."[3] Trollope's indictment on nineteenth-century preaching still rings true. Congregations often languish through sermons simply because the communication fails to hold their attention and induces a state of comatose boredom. It doesn't have to be that way!

If audience boredom is the disease, then communication predictability is a major cause of the disease. Nothing spreads audience boredom like a communication style that is stagnant and predictable. John Killinger writes, "Considering how many sermons most preachers deliver in a lifetime, it's easy to understand how sermons fall into formulas and patterns, and thus become *predictable*. But *predictability* kills interest."[4] This seemed obvious to me.

But multisensory communication is quintessentially *unpredictable* and filled with *variety*. It is the antithesis of falling into a communication rut. The wonder of multisensory communication lies not only in its power to engage multiple senses, but also in its capacity to be diverse and changing. The very nature of multisensory teaching keeps it out of ruts, formulas, and patterns.

The question, however, that was keeping me awake at night was this: Does multisensory communication translate into higher attention levels in our audiences and less audience boredom? Could such a correlation be validated?

THE CRYSTAL CLEAR EFFECT

In the movie *A Few Good Men*, Jack Nicholson plays the role of Colonel Nathan Jessup. While on a witness stand, he asks a Navy lawyer, played by Tom Cruise, a question about intellectual comprehension: "Are we clear?"

Cruise responds, "Yes."

Nicholson shouts the question again, "Are we clear?"

In one of those classic Hollywood moments, Tom Cruise responds. "Crystal." The point is this: Crystal clear communication translates into crystal clear comprehension.

Many people say they come to Christ Fellowship specifically because the multisensory style of communication makes information *clear — crystal clear*. The verbal, visual, and interactive teaching adds up to better *comprehension* for them. All three teaching pastors — Eric Geiger, Tony Isaacs, and myself — teach in a multisensory form, and people continually tells us it is what they need in order to best understand the teaching.

But, once again, my question was this: Does multisensory communication really add up to higher levels of audience comprehension? I was hearing anecdotal testimonies, but could these testimonies be verified? Was it just subjective, or could it be tested and demonstrated to be objective fact?

As teachers, we must communicate in a form that is clear. Nothing is more frustrating for a church audience than sitting through a sermon they don't understand. If you leave them in the fog too many times, they will not return. Moreover, if the audience fails to comprehend the message we teach, it will be impossible for them to be "doers of the Word" we teach.

In other words, *audience comprehension demands teacher clarity*. If multisensory communication can make our communication clearer, then common sense says we must consider its usage.

THE UNFORGETTABLE EFFECT

As I observed in the three multisensory cases noted above, there was another common denominator: *high retention* in the congregation. It is what I refer to as *the unforgettable effect*. Debbie's teaching seemed unforgettable; Tony's teaching seemed unforgettable; and my own multisensory teaching seemed to linger long in the minds of Christ Fellowship — much longer than my traditional lecture deliveries. But was my perception based in reality? I was hearing testimonies of the unforgettable effect, but could such an effect be proven in a laboratory test?

As teachers of the Word, our mission is to etch biblical truth into the minds of our congregation. We want them to remember the truths we teach, so they can meditate on it and apply it to their lives. However, how can they act on what they don't remember?

Let us never forget that much of our teaching is very forgettable. We can't even remember it ourselves sometimes, much less our congregation. Can multisensory communication change that? Can multisensory communication make our teaching less forgettable and more memorable?

VALIDATING THE EFFECT

There *appeared* to be a correlation between the number of senses that were being stirred by the teachers and the learning levels of those who were being taught. I call this *the multisensory effect*: The more senses the teacher stirs in the audience, the higher the levels of audience attention, comprehension, and retention. I had a *hunch*, but could I *prove* it? Moreover, if people have higher levels of *attention*, if they have higher levels of *understanding*, and if they can *remember* what we teach, is there also a higher probability that they will actually *do* what we teach?

Let's go back to the morning when I watched Tony Isaacs teaching at Christ Fellowship. As I watched Tony speak and observed the reaction of the congregation, a logical formula began developing in my mind. I scratched it on the back of a church bulletin:

Verbal clarity + Visual aids + Interaction = Maximum Learning

But was this an accurate formula for teaching in churches? Do congregational learning levels rise when we combine verbal clarity with visual aids? Do they rise even more when we add audience interaction? So far, all I had was anecdotal experiences but no definitive evidence for the multisensory effect. This is what researchers refer to as *casual observation*. But I wanted to know for certain whether there was a verifiable relationship between multisensory teaching and congregational learning. I wanted objective proof.

Working alongside my doctoral (EdD) advisors at Southern Baptist Theological Seminary in Louisville, Kentucky, we came up with a research design that would either validate the effect of multisensory teaching or invalidate it. The experiment would seek to determine if multisensory teaching outperforms lecture in terms of the effect on congregational attention, comprehension, and retention. In other words, do learning levels increase when sensory stimulation increases?

As the senior pastor of Christ Fellowship in Miami, Florida, I had the perfect context in which to do research and to test the multisensory teaching theory. Christ Fellowship is a multicultural megachurch. At the time I conducted the research, we had members from sixty-one different nationalities (presently we have seventy-six). Speaking at Christ Fellowship feels like speaking before a United Nations assembly. The worship may be as close to the scene of Revelation 5:9 as one can get on this earth: "from every tribe and language and people and nation." This audience offered me an ideal test population:

- I had a large congregation.
- The test sample encompassed adults from sixty-one different nationalities.
- I had a cross section of race, age, and culture.
- I had three services to test three different teaching methodologies.
- I had tremendous video and technological resources at my disposal.

Many similar research projects proceed with much smaller audience samples. Such research, if conducted thoroughly and with integrity, is respected among researchers. A smaller sample population limits the application that can be made to other learning contexts. But by having all the features listed above, application of the findings can be applied to a wider scale.

THE TEST

In order to test the effects of multisensory teaching, three types of sermon delivery were planned. The *content* would be the same in all three sermons, but the *delivery* techniques would be different. The three communication techniques were referred to as:

Verbal: lecture style teaching delivered in a *verbal form*, which consequently connects only to the congregation's sense of *hearing*.

Verbal + Visual: teaching delivered in a *verbal + visual form*, which consequently connects to the congregation's sense of *hearing* and *seeing*.

Verbal + Visual + Interactive: Teaching delivered in a *verbal + visual + interactive form*, which consequently connects to the congregation's sense of *hearing, seeing*, and *touch*.

To evaluate the effectiveness of these three teaching styles, we created a series of tests that would measure attention levels, comprehension levels, and retention levels. The test was conducted three times to ensure reliability. We assembled a team of professors, pastors, and other educators to oversee the experiment and to ensure accuracy and integrity.

After doing the three styles of preaching, we measured and compared *attention levels, comprehension levels*, and *retention levels* between the teaching styles. It was during this research that we could draw conclusions about the multisensory effect as a powerful form of teaching.

To be straightforward with the reader, we anticipated better learning scores among those who were taught using multisensory communication. We had a hunch that multisensory teaching would outperform lecture delivery. The effect, however, was more powerful than we imagined. The learning differences between those exposed to lecture and those treated with multisensory communication was astonishing! Our statistician told us that what we had found was *highly significant*!

Later in this book, we will discuss further how this research was conducted and how the results unfolded, but here's the watercooler conversation. Those who were treated with multisensory communication clearly had higher levels of *attention*, higher levels of *understanding*, and longer lasting *memory* of what was taught. In fact, the difference was so great that the results came in mostly at the .001 level.

Let me quote my friend and ministry colleague Eric Geiger about these kinds of findings: "When a researcher discovers a relationship at the .05 level, he calls a friend and brags about it. When he finds something at the .01 levels, he calls his publicist and prepares to write a book. Finding something at the .001 level does not happen often. If you're a stats person, it's called highly significant!"

Simply put, the effect of multisensory communication is increased levels of congregational *attention*, *comprehension*, and *retention*, which can then translate into higher *application* of the sermon. In other words, *learning* the Word and *doing* the Word are accelerated when people hear the sermon, see the sermon, and interact with the sermon, as opposed to just hearing it. For you visual learners, the effect adds up like this:

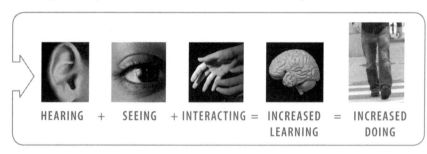

HEARING   +   SEEING   + INTERACTING = INCREASED   =   INCREASED
LEARNING   DOING

INCREASING EFFECTIVENESS

When I began experimenting with multisensory communication in 2001, I had been a pastor-teacher for twenty years. Frankly, I thought I had maxed out my ability as a communicator. Mind you, I had won an award for preaching while in Bible College, and I had continued to hone my verbal skills and homiletic delivery. But by my own calculations, by the year 2000, I had reached the limit on my communication skills. I had settled in to finish my teaching ministry as a fairly good communicator.

Again, was I in for a shock. As you will see in the following chapter, my communication effectiveness rose significantly when I switched from lecture to multisensory communication. In all three dimensions (attention, comprehension, and retention) my effectiveness rose remarkably. In fact, the average comprehension, and retention levels in the congregation rose 66.5 percent when I used dual sensory communication (verbal and visual) and 76.1 percent when I used multisensory (verbal + visual + interactive). A baseball player who raises his batting average 76.1 percent would move from a good hitter to a great hitter or from great to phenomenal!

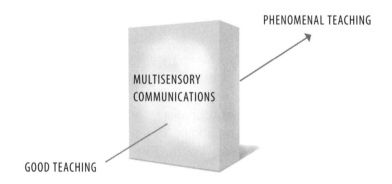

Multisensory communication has that kind of impact. Mind you, I did not become a better *speaker*; I became a better *communicator*. I still had the same speaking talent I had always had. It was not my communication talent that elevated the results; it was the communication technique. Whether you are a good communicator or a great communicator, multisensory delivery can significantly elevate your effectiveness as a biblical communicator.

MANY PASTOR-TEACHERS KNOW THE EFFECT

Many pastors who have a passion to teach the Word of God understand the power of multisensory teaching. That's why they use it. As pastors, our calling is to *teach*. Needless to say, effective teaching necessitates effective communication. Stated another way: Great teachers are great communicators.

Pastor-teachers who employee multisensory communication do so not to be trendy, but to be more effective. They understand that the people in their congregation have different styles in which they prefer to learn, and they understand one style of teaching does not fit everyone in their congregation. In order to connect to all the audience as opposed to only a portion of it, they teach in a multisensory form.

Conferences on how to use multisensory communication as a means of elevating teaching impact are becoming widespread. Below are two of the more prominent biblical multisensory teachers who have blazed the trail.

Andy Stanley. Andy Stanley began North Point Community Church in Alpharetta, Georgia, in 1995. Prior to this, he had served as Youth Pastor at First Baptist Church of Atlanta, where his father, Charles Stanley, serves

Andy Stanley

as senior pastor. As a youth pastor, Andy was given the latitude to use many techniques to communicate to his youth. He effectively used visual aids and interactive methodologies in his teaching.

Many view such strategies as acceptable for youth, but they see them as unacceptable for teaching in an adult context, especially in worship. Stanley decided to break with that traditional view and use the same multisensory teaching he had employed as a youth pastor in his new start at North Point Community Church. Consequently, Andy's personal style of communication and his passion to make it captivating, clear, and memorable have resulted in the church's explosive growth.

It seems odd that some think it is legitimate to use such teaching techniques with children and youth, but consider it illegitimate to bring such creativity into the adult context. Reg Grant of Dallas Theological Seminary writes, "Young children rely on anything that helps them communicate their ideas — stories, anecdotes, sticks, rocks — whatever lies at hand. As adults, now, we regard those natural elements of persuasion as foreign matter, alien fragments of a world before formal education. What happened?"[5]

Kerry Shook. Kerry Shook is an imaginative and unpredictable preacher. Beginning with eight people, he now sees 15,000 people attend Fellowship of the Woodlands on weekends, and some pack an extra pair of shoes.

Several years ago, Shook learned from area shelters that shoes and underwear were the two biggest needs of homeless people. After preaching a sermon about the poor, Shook challenged attendees to leave their shoes on the platform if they felt led to do so. By the time the weekend services were finished, the church had collected more than 4,500 pairs of shoes.

Kerry Shook

Talk about unpredictable! Talk about verbal, visual, and interactive communication!

SIGNIFICANT EFFECTS OF MULTISENSORY PREACHING
On Church Growth at Christ Fellowship in Miami

There is a mosaic of factors that have contributed to the numerical and spiritual growth at Christ Fellowship. I am convinced that the multisensory teaching style of the pastor-teachers is one of those factors.

Let me give a little history. I became senior pastor of Christ Fellowship in 1996. Initially, the church experienced some growth, but then the growth rate reached a plateau. As the lead pastor-teacher, I was committed to the exposition of Scripture, which I am still convinced carries the highest potency of biblical teaching. Christ Fellowship, however, seemed to stagnate numerically.

Then, along with the other teaching pastors, we began teaching in a multisensory form. We began combining verbal clarity with visual aids and interactive teaching. Initially, our goal for changing methods of teaching had nothing to do with church growth. We only wanted to elevate attention levels, comprehension levels, and retention levels of what we were teaching. Miami-Dade is the second most unchurched county in America, and consequently grabbing attention and being clear are nonnegotiable.

We immediately began to see the effects on grabbing people's attention and increasing comprehension and retention. But the surprise factor that never crossed our mind was the church growth factor. Shortly after combining exposition with multisensory communication, we began to experience substantial church growth. This year, Christ Fellowship is listed number eighty-one among the hundred fastest growing churches in America. We are also listed in the top one hundred baptisms in our denomination.

Among the montage of strategies and blessings that have contributed to the growth at Christ Fellowship, three stand out. First, we remained loyal to Bible exposition. Second, we became simpler in our discipleship process (see *Simple Church* by Eric Geiger). Finally, we embraced the multisensory method of teaching the Scriptures to our people. I am persuaded that these three dynamics are greatly responsible for the blessings of God at Christ Fellowship.

On the Multicultural Church

One of the great blessings of pastoring a church in the city of Miami is the diversity. Miami is a melting pot of cultures, races, and beliefs. Some see that kind of diversity as a curse. Others see it as an unbreechable obstacle. Christ Fellowship, however, has chosen to embrace that diversity as a gift from God. Each weekend, we celebrate the tapestry of color and culture that so defines who we are as a people of God. Incidentally, if prognosticators are accurate in their view of the future, your church will need to become more like Christ Fellowship. You too will need to embrace the diversity that so blesses this great country of ours.

There are, however, some challenges. One of the great challenges is the challenge of cross-cultural communication. In Miami, we are not communicating to a mission field of one culture; we are communicating to a mission field with multiple cultures. A missionary friend serving in a foreign country recently told me that it is much easier to reach people of one nationality on the mission field than it is to reach a multicultural context such as Miami.

Every weekend at Christ Fellowship, there are seventy-plus nationalities of people — people who have learned to process information in a myriad of ways. We must communicate in a form that is sensitive to those needs, and multisensory communication has helped us do that. Communication and mission expert David Hesselgrave underscores this idea when he writes:

> It is not just *who* says *what* to *whom*, but *how* the message is channeled to the respondent that determines how the message will be decoded. Language is basic to communication, but language does not stand-alone. As we have said, words are augmented by pictures, actions, sounds, silence, smells, and objects.[6]

I have no way of testing my observations for absolute proof, but I can offer what I believe is self-evident: Verbal clarity, combined with the support of visual aids, creativity, and interactive communication, has been a blessing from God. I am convinced it has helped us communicate across the multiple cultures that so define Miami.

On the Unchurched

Miami is a different ball game in terms of reaching the lost. In a demographic taken when I first came to Christ Fellowship, the statistics revealed that only 7 percent of the population in our ten-mile radius considered themselves to be Protestant. I quickly realized, "Dorothy, we're not in Kansas any more." I was no longer pastoring a church in a Bible Belt environment.

If people were going to come to Christ Fellowship, they would not be coming here in terms of transfering from other churches. People would have to be reached on the streets, invited to church, and communicated to in a style that was captivating and crystal clear. I am convinced that combining the power of the Word with a clear process of communication has enabled us to reach people in this largely unchurched city.

Recently, I invited my new, unchurched neighbors to church. They decided to attend one of our weekend services, and they met the Lord in a personal and intimate way. In my subsequent conversation with them, one of the factors they mentioned was the way the multisensory communication helped them understand the message. As we will see later, Jesus used all sorts of visuals and interactive elements to connect to the lost, so why shouldn't we?

On a Sensory-Dependent World

Recently, my wife was on an airplane flying from Miami to Charlotte, North Carolina. In the seat next to her was a teenage boy, and he was playing with a multisensory device called a Gameboy™. The electronic toy combines verbal, visual, and interactive elements. Rhonda was amazed, not with the device itself, but the power with which it held this boy's attention. He rarely looked up. The verbal, visual, and interactive game absorbed his attention for the entire two-hour flight.

Modern technology has definitely become more and more multisensory in its communication. We can see the increased stimulation of the senses by looking at the technological progression from radio, to television, to computers.

- The radio is strictly monosensory in its communication — hearing only.
- The television is dual sensory — hearing and seeing.
- The computer is multisensory — hearing, seeing, and interacting.

As I thought about how totally absorbed this boy was with his device, I was reminded of recent research. Some neurological and cognitive experts believe multisensory technology has created a multisensory-dependent culture. In other words, modern technology has made many people in our culture *dependent on more than one sense*. Such people struggle to pay attention unless the teaching is presented in a form that fits their lives.

Researchers believe early exposure to television and other forms of communication technologies have generated the onset of this dependency. For example, recent neurological research links attention deficiency in children to early exposure to television watching. In fact, according to a study from the Children's Hospital and Regional Medical Center in Seattle, early television exposure in children ages one to three is associated with attention problems by age seven. Recent conclusions from the research indicate that television may overstimulate and permanently rewire the developing brain to be visually dependent when it comes to attention span. A group of researchers wrote, "We hypothesize that very early exposure to television during the critical periods of synaptic development would be associated with subsequent attention problems."[7]

In other words, many people who sit in our congregation, especially the younger people, have brains that are neurologically rewired and neurologically dependent on multisensory teaching. Their minds *require* multisensory teaching for maximum attention, comprehension, and retention. Pastors, Christian teachers, and others who communicate the Word must come to terms with this reality. The great preacher John Stott has acknowledged this dependency and the problems it poses for pastors: "Television makes it harder for people to listen attentively and responsively, and therefore for preachers to hold a congregation's attention."[8]

Anyone who seeks to teach must embrace these neurological facts. Pastors and teachers may wish that their students were more auditory, but the fact is that many are visual and interactive learners. We may wish they were able to learn from our lectures, but the fact is, many cannot. They need to hear our teaching, see our teaching, and interact with it for maximum learning. Multisensory communication meets this multisensory need.

THE "SPECIAL EFFECT" — EFFECT

Multisensory communication does for preaching what special effects have done for movies; it makes the presentation more graphic. Some people imagine that multisensory communication "waters down" the message of the gospel. The truth is, it fires it up! In my own preaching, the use of multisensory communication has made theological truths more vivid and more explicit. It's interesting that I have never been accused of making my preaching too weak. I have, however, been accused of making it too explicit. That's the power of multisensory communication.

A classic example of this is the effect of the movie *The Passion of the Christ*. Like many pastors, I was invited to a sneak preview of the movie before it was released. I have to admit that I was suspicious of anything Hollywood produces about our Savior. Was I in for a shock! Mind you, I had read about the crucifixion of Christ, I had taught on the subject in great detail, I had *heard* great theologians teach on it, and I had wept while *hearing* about his suffering.

But when I *saw* the crucifixion in dramatic form, my reaction was remarkably different. As I sat there in the theatre and *heard* the flogging, *saw* the blood splatter, and *felt* the thunder of God in the room, I was absolutely broken! During the flogging scene, I wanted to scream out, "Stop!" Hearing it, seeing it, and feeling it made me feel as if I were immersed in the scene. The difference between hearing about it and experiencing it was like the difference between night and day.

That's the effect of multisensory teaching. In no way does it tone down the message. Rather, it turns up the heat. It provides picturesque detail and gives explosive impact. Multisensory communication lets the audience hear, see, interact, and experience the Word of God.

WATCH THE EFFECT FOR YOURSELF

Sometimes you have to measure two things to determine if there is a difference. There are other times when it is obvious. In these pictures, no one really needs to measure the effects to know a difference exists. The picture of Jarred to the left shows his weight when exposed to an unhealthy diet. The opposing picture shows Jarred after treatment with a lowfat diet. The difference is self-evident. No one needs to say, "Step on the scales and let's see if you have lost weight." We may not know his exact weight, but the side-by-side observation shows a remarkable difference in the diet effect.

Jarred before and after diet.

In the next chapter, we will measure the differences between lecture teaching and multisensory teaching as it occurred at Christ Fellowship. The reader needs to know, however, that we did not have to measure attention levels to know there was a difference. It was obvious. You could see the difference. You could see it in the posture of the people. You could see it in their faces. You could hear it in the conversations.

Perhaps the best way for you to know the power of multisensory preaching is to test this effect for yourself. I recommend you do a side-by-side test. Preach lecture in one service and multisensory in the next. The difference will be clear and present. Prepare to be blown away. In the following chapters, I am going to stack up the experimental evidence, the neurological facts, and the theological truth. But there's nothing like seeing it for yourself.

A CAUTIONARY NOTE

I'm not saying, of course, that pastors should use this method of communication as if it were some sort of biblical mandate from God. I am saying that it can elevate your communication effect. It can boost levels of attention in your congregation, and it can increase congregational levels of comprehension and retention.

I am not saying that visual aids and interaction should dominate the sermon. In fact, let me be clear. Textual accuracy is the most critical portion of biblical teaching. Second to that is the need for verbal clarity. Sound biblical teaching must begin with sound exegesis followed by verbal clarity. Visual aids and interaction with the audience should be viewed as aids to that process. Multisensory communication is not the end; it is only a means to the end. The end goal is to produce "doers of the Word" through higher levels of attention, comprehension, and retention.

I must confess that I have witnessed multisensory teaching that had the appearance of a sideshow. In those cases, the multisensory elements took over the biblical message and also took away from its effect. Too much of a good thing can actually distract our audience away from the Word we are seeking to teach. That is not what we are advocating here. In the right hands, it can be a tool to help us in making disciples for our Lord. In the wrong hands, it can cheapen the message and steal the glory that belongs to God.

DISCUSSION QUESTIONS

1. Do you remember any preachers or teachers in your past who taught you using multisensory communication? Did they use visuals, and if so, how did you respond to that? Was the teaching interactive, and if so, how did you respond?

2. Describe your communication style:
   - Predictable and unchanging
   - Unpredictable and varying

3. What is the status of your communication effectiveness in the past few years?
   - I am improving my communication skills.
   - My communication skills have plateaued.

4. In our culture, in what ways have you seen people respond to multisensory communication?

CHAPTER 3

EXPECT: DRAMATIC RESULTS

There is no way to understand the world without first detecting it through the radar of our senses.

DIANE ACKERMAN

Hank Aaron, power hitter for the Atlanta Braves, came to bat against the New York Yankees. Behind the plate catching was Yankee great, Yogi Berra. As Hank stepped into the batter's box, Yogi decided to confuse Hank by attempting to distract him from the ball. He wanted to get Hank's eye off the ball by messing with his head.

Hank Aaron

Yogi said, "Hank, you're holding the bat wrong. You're supposed to be able to *read* the trademark on the bat. Can you *read* it, Hank? You've got the bat backwards, that's why you can't *read* it."

On the very next pitch, Hank drove the ball into the left field seats for a home run, and he began circling the bases. Yogi was left standing at home plate with mask in one hand, glove in the other, looking dejected. As Hank rounded the bases and crossed home plate, he looked at Yogi, and said, "Hey, Yogi, I didn't come here to *read*."[1]

Hank Aaron was a great hitter because he understood his objective as a batter. He knew *why* he was in the batter's box, and he knew what he was there to accomplish. He didn't come to the batter's box to *read*. He didn't come to talk. He came there to *hit* the ball, cross home plate, and score runs. That was his objective, and he stayed focused on it.

GREAT BIBLE TEACHERS
They Know Their Objectives

In my research, I have found that great Bible teachers are like Hank Aaron. When they step into the "teacher's box," they know *why* they are there and *what* they are supposed to accomplish. They are *not* there just to be heard. They are *not* there just to impart information. They *are* there to produce "doers of the Word." That is the objective given to them by God, and they stay focused on it.

"Do not merely listen to the word, and so deceive yourselves. Do what it says," says James (James 1:22). In the mind of a great Bible teacher, crossing home plate happens only when the audience *does* what has been taught.

Realizing the objective is to produce "doers of the Word," great Bible teachers step up to the plate with that objective in mind. They predetermine what a particular text calls the audience to do, and they are obsessed with getting them to do it. They can define the objective, articulate the objective, and drive that objective all the way to home plate.

Conversely, many Bible teachers and preachers step into the teacher's box with no audience goal in mind. They have no idea what they want the audience to do. It's as if their only goal is to be heard. They explain the Greek, Hebrew, and Aramaic; they pontificate on the historical background of the text; they line up the sermon in the correct homiletic style; but they have no idea what they want people to *do*. No disrespect intended, but who needs to hear you talk? Who doesn't need a life changed by God?

Granted, teaching without having clear audience goals is safe and predictable, but it is also impotent. Few people have embraced biblical preaching more than Dr. Walter Kaiser. Yet, after giving a passionate call for expository preaching, he gives this warning: "Nothing can be more dreary and grind the soul and spirit of the church than the dry recounting of Biblical episodes apparently unrelated to the present."[2]

Likewise, Joe Stowell has this to say about such aimless preaching: "Preaching to convey information is predictable and unthreatening. Preaching to effect transformation is hard work and risky business. Yet that is the whole point of preaching. An effective sermon is measured not by its polished technique but by the ability of the preacher to connect the Word to the reality of the listener's life."[3] Producing "doers of the Word" is "home plate" for great teachers and they obsess over it.

They Know the Base Path to Action

Great teachers not only view producing "doers of the Word" as home plate, they also know the base path that leads to producing such doers. The communication path for leading your audience to action is a lot like taking them around a baseball diamond. A three-base sequence of communication leads to congregation action. Educators refer to this sequence as *Bloom's taxonomy of learning objectives*.[4] Let's observe a visual of this sequence.

If audience *action* is viewed as the *home plate*, then there are three cognitive bases that must first be crossed. Just as no base runner ever crosses home plate without first crossing first, second, and third base, no teacher can get his or her audience to action without first getting them to cross the bases of *attention*, *comprehension*, and *retention*.

First base in the communication sequence is gaining audience *attention*. An audience that has not paid attention will be hard-pressed to apply what they have been taught. If the teacher loses the battle for attention, he or she loses the war for action.

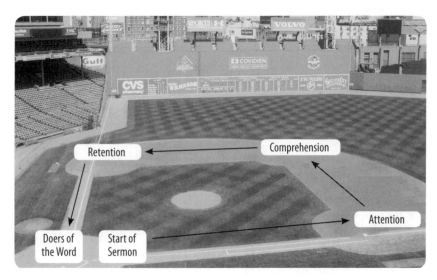

Second base in the communication sequence is audience *comprehension*. Comprehension asks: Did the audience understand what was being communicated? Was it crystal clear? It is not enough for the congregation to be mentally engaged to the teaching; they must mentally comprehend the teaching. An audience will not be able to act on what they do not understand.

Third base is audience *retention*. Retention asks: Will the audience remember what was taught? Retention is the "aftereffect" of learning that makes recall possible. Effective teaching is memorable and recallable. It is impossible for people to act on what they cannot remember.

Home plate is crossed when our audience or congregation actually does what we have taught them from the Word.

They Shepherd the Audience around the Bases

The difference between a *good* teacher and a *great* teacher is the great teacher knows how to shepherd the audience around those bases. In fact, the great teacher actually plans the message with that sequence in mind.

First, great teachers strategically plan how to gain audience *attention*. They plan ahead of time how to grab the minds of the audience and shepherd them to first base. Nothing is left to chance. In fact, great teachers expend great amounts energy at the outset of the teaching to ensure the audience is mentally engaged. They cannot bear the thought of boring the audience.

Second, great teachers make certain the message is *understandable*. They plan the teaching and deliver in a form that makes it easy to grasp. Great teachers don't want the teaching to be merely clear, they want it to be crystal clear! Even if the subject is complex and difficult to understand, great teachers force it to be understandable through a calculated method of delivery.

Third, the great teacher is not satisfied with just being understood, they are obsessive about being *remembered*. They plot the delivery of their teaching and communicate it in a fashion that is unforgettable.

Only after the teacher takes his audience to first, second, and third bases can the audience be led to home. This ability is what separates the good from the great.

Don't miss what I am about to write, because it is essential to being a great teacher or preacher. You must teach in a form that *attracts attention* (first base), that *is understandable* (second base), and that *is memorable* (third base). Failure at any one of those bases will stop you short of home plate.

Here's the $9.99 question (half the price of the book): Will multisensory teaching help you get more of your people to home plate? If you adopt a multisensory style of communication, will it be more than adopting some latest fad that comes and goes? Or is there hard evidence showing that it will actually help you become more captivating, more understandable, and more memorable? The evidence of our research gives a resounding "yes" to these questions.

THE RESEARCH
Factors that Lead to This Research

Two factors led to the launch of this research and the experiments that followed. The first was the effect I was seeing with my own eyes. I could not ignore the multisensory effect I was noticing at Christ Fellowship. As I spoke with other pastors who were teaching in a multisensory form, they gave the same testimony. Though they had no concrete evidence to support what they were observing, they too knew multisensory communication was highly effective. Their success, their excitement, and the growth of their churches compelled me to seek proof for the effect of multisensory communication.

The second factor was the frustration I was hearing from pastors and teachers of the Word. At the time of the research, I was teaching expository preaching at a local seminary, and I was constantly running into pastors and students who were good communicators, but who needed to move their communication capacity to a higher level. Their average communication skill was keeping their churches at average levels of growth, both spiritually and numerically.

Let's face the music: We can take innumerable seminars on church growth, but if we cannot communicate to our congregation in a way that moves them to action, it is futile. If we cannot communicate in a form that is captivating and motivating, we will continue to be frustrated with our churches.

Our tendency, then, will be to blame the congregation for their "lack of love for God" rather than to evaluate our own teaching effectiveness. I hear that reaction all the time. "The reason my church fails to grow is because there needs to be a revival in the hearts of the people. It's their fault!" Blaming our congregation is much easier than taking a hard look at our own effectiveness as communicators.

But for those pastors who want to work on their own side of the ledger, I am convinced that multisensory communication can elevate us from good communicators to phenomenal communicators — the kind of biblical communication that will captivate our audiences and move people around the bases to become doers of the Word.

Launching the Test

The goal of the test was simple: to see if multisensory communication could help pastors and Christian teachers be more effective communicators. Could multisensory communication outperform lecture communication in terms of audience attention, comprehension, and retention?

I won't bore you with mountains of sleep-inducing research language, but I must make some bold statements. The research was conducted thoroughly and the research design was reliable. While we don't claim inerrancy for the test, the advisors assisting in the experiment strongly agreed as to how the test should proceed.

For you research lovers, the methodology for measuring attention, comprehension, and retention was a *quasi-experimental design*. It was modeled after the design in the Leedy and Ormord's text, *Practical Research: Planning and Design*.[5] The exception was that we were working with a much larger and a much more diverse sample population. By having a large audience to test with adults from sixty-one different nationalities, application of the findings can be applied to a much wider scale. The experiments consisted of three Quasi-Experimental Post-test Only Control Group Designs. The independent variable was the teaching methodologies and the dependent variable was the effect on audience attention, comprehension, and retention.

To measure audience comprehension and retention levels, a fill-in-the-blank test was given at the conclusion of the final week of treatment. Questions (about not well-known facts) were designed to determine the congregation's understanding and memory of material taught during the three types of delivery. Those delivery types were:

Verbal
Verbal + visual
Verbal + visual + interactive

Data was subsequently gathered to determine the relationship between the teaching methodologies to audience comprehension and retention.

To measure audience *attention* levels, observations were conducted. Mind you, attention levels can be determined simply by comparing comprehension and retention scores. However, we wanted something more concrete than that. We measured congregational attention levels by observing their eye contact with the teacher — that is, by *attraction* to the teacher or *distraction* from the teacher.

The test for attention levels was modeled after experiments conducted by Phye and Andre.[6] We measured audience attention levels by observing random areas of the audience with high-resolution cameras. Video observations were taken both during the verbal sermons and during the multisensory sermons.

A panel performed post-treatment analysis of the videotapes. Each person in the frame was observed and marked when eye contact was distracted away from the teacher. This was tedious work, and I am grateful for the labor of this panel. Data was subsequently gathered to determine the relationship between teaching methodologies and audience attention.

The goal was to compare attention levels when the congregation was exposed to lecture communication and when they were exposed to multisensory communication. Would levels increase when more senses were stimulated? That was the question we were seeking to answer. Let's look at the bases of attention, comprehension, and retention; at the end of each, we will present the results of our research.

GAIN ATTENTION: MAKING IT TO FIRST BASE

The first important step, as already stated, is to capture attention. Failure to capture attention is like being thrown out at first. You're out!

What is attention? Simply stated, attention means the attraction of the

mind upon some object. Put negatively, inattention means the distraction of the mind away from that object. If we want people to act on what we teach, we must communicate in a form that motivates them to give us their undivided attention.

From the moment you launch your sermon, you

have only seconds to grab the audience's attention. With each second that you fail to grab their attention, it becomes more and more difficult to do so. In fact, if you have not grabbed audience attention within a few minutes, they are already starting to turn you off. They turn their attention away from you, and their mind flits away to other things. We should realize too that many unsaved people are already predisposed to think the Bible is boring. Once we begin the communication process, we only have seconds to change their mind.

The History Channel television program *Seconds from Disaster* documents the step-by-step failures that have led to major disasters such as airplane crashes, space shuttle disasters, and so on. Every time I see that program, I am reminded of the step-by-step failures that lead to communication disasters. Most communication disasters in the pulpit happen in those first moments of the introduction.

Every time we step up to teach, many of the people in the congregation are having mental wars in their heads. Some are mentally tired from a hard week at work, and they will struggle just to stay awake. Others are angry, perhaps because of an argument that ensued on the way to church. Many are preoccupied with job issues, finances, or other forces that have them worried and upset.

As you step into the batter's box to teach, you will literally have to wrestle for control of their attention. It's not that they don't love God; it's just that their minds have a deadening fatigue of weariness. These people desperately need to hear from God, but you will have only moments to gain their attention. Engage them quickly, or you will strike out.

The Heartache of "Striking Out"

Few things are more demoralizing than not being able to attract the attention of our audience. It is even more disheartening when we feel we are "boring" our audience while teaching the most powerful book in the world. Yet many pastors feel that way week after week. Haddon Robinson, professor of preaching at Gordon Conwell Theological Seminary, recounts this heart-wrenching episode:

> The pastor slumped down in his seat opposite me in the restaurant and played with the water glass. Then he made a comment that sounded like a confession. "I am bored, very bored with my own preaching." What surprised me, though, was how he put it. He wasn't saying, "I'm afraid I'm boring my congregation." He was admitting something even more deadening: "I am boring myself with my own preaching."[7]

I cannot imagine the heartache that pastor must have been feeling. To "bore" yourself with your own preaching is reason enough to resign from the ministry. The heartbeat of this book is to help such pastors and other Christian teachers. The passion behind this book is to demonstrate that it is not just communication *talent* that matters; it is communication *techniques* that matter. We may not be able to alter natural talent, but we can alter techniques that will improve our communication impact. By moving from pure lecture to multisensory communication, all preachers can be more effective at reaching first base, that is, by attracting audience attention.

Are They "Totally Absorbed" with Your Teaching?

When it comes to attention, I don't have to tell you that there are different levels of attention. Attention is not a static condition. Attention levels range from *flitting,* to *passive,* to *absorption. Flitting attention* is when a person is attentive for a moment, but then attention flits away like a bird to something else.

Passive attention is when someone is paying attention to you, but his or her mind is on autopilot. They are paying attention, but they are not absorbed in the subject.

Absorption is a totally different level of attention. People will say an individual is *totally absorbed* in something. That means the object has the person's full attention and is occupying the whole of the consciousness. The person is so fixed on the object that almost nothing can break his or her concentration.

Let me give you an idea of absorption. Last month I was in a Best Buy store looking at plasma TVs. While there, I witnessed *total absorption.* It was July 4, and at the same time I was in the store, it was time for the space shuttle to blast off from Cape Kennedy in Florida. Several guys and myself gathered into the high tech media room. The room screamed multisensory communication. The plasma TV was high definition. It boasted a sixty-inch screen with a powerful surround sound package.

The countdown went to zero and an enormous explosion of light and sound rocked the room. None of us spoke, and not one of us took our eyes off the shuttle. As the shuttle cleared the tower and was rocketing into the deep blue skies, one guy's wife stepped into the room and called for him. He never even acknowledged her. In frustration she yelled at him, "Hector!" He never took his eyes off the screen, and neither did I. That is what it means to be *totally absorbed.*

Total absorption is the level of attention we should attract as we lead people into the Holy of Holies of God's Word. Multisensory communication can help us garner that level of attention. In the book of Hebrews, God demands total absorption when considering Jesus Christ. "We must pay more careful attention, therefore, to what we have heard, so that we do not drift away" (Hebrews 2:1). The phrase "pay more careful attention" translates a graphic Greek term that has to do with one's level of attention: *prosecho*. The core of this word is the verb *echo*, which means "to hold something," sometimes in one's mind.[8] The prefix *pros* generally means "before."[9] *Prosecho*, then, means "to hold something before one's mind" or "to pay attention to something."[10] This is the antithesis of a "drifting mind" or a "divided mind." When it comes to hearing the message of Christ, the writer of Hebrews is saying, "We must be totally absorbed in the message."

The same idea is captured in Hebrews 3:1: "Therefore, holy brothers, who share in the heavenly calling, fix your thoughts on Jesus." The phrase "fix your thoughts" is a translation of the compound Greek word *katanoeo*. *Katanoeo* means "to direct one's whole mind to an object." J. Behm says it denotes "intellectual absorption"; it means "to immerse oneself and hence to apprehend."[11] That kind of absorption and immersion is what we should strive for as we teach the Word of God.

God makes no apology in demanding *total absorption*. "Again Jesus called the crowd to him and said, '*Listen* to me, everyone, and understand this'" (Mark 7:14, italics added). Not only did Jesus not apologize for demanding attention, he used every means possible to be sure he got it. Roy Zuck, professor at Dallas Theological Seminary, says: "To motivate, be sure you capture the student's attention at the very outset. Jesus did this effectively ... by telling stories, asking questions, and *using visuals*."[12]

Captivating Communication = Total Absorption

Generally speaking, individuals learn most easily and most economically when they are absorbed in the learning process. We learn most effectively when the teaching attracts us by its own right, when it is so captivating that it carries us with it — so to speak. Let us bring that into the worship center where you and I teach. The congregation that is sitting on the edge of their seats is the congregation that will learn the easiest and the best. Learning for them is an exciting and enjoyable experience.

This is the antithesis of the person who is bored to tears and whose mind is flitting to other thoughts while we teach the precious Word. What teacher himself has not read through an entire page of material only to get to the end of the page and realize he or she has not absorbed a single thought from the page? When your congregation is totally absorbed in your teaching, they will not experience such mental dead spots.

It has been my experience that multisensory communication grabs attention if used early in the sermon. We either captivate people early in the sermon, or we lose them. We have only moments at the beginning of the message to hook them and carry them along for the learning process. Because the launch of the sermon is the most crucial moment, this is where the most energy must be invested. We will say more about this in part 3, but suffice it for now to say, "Put your best hitters at the beginning of the sermon." Make it verbal, visual, and interactive.

Attention Test Results

The question we were seeking to answer here in our test research was this: Does multisensory communication outperform lecture communication in terms of *attracting audience attention*? The results of our test research have confirmed that it does indeed. The attention portion of the research design compared audience attention levels in three separate tests. In each test, the audience was treated with lecture delivery in one message and multisensory in the other. Observations were made, data was gathered, and the results were plotted side by side.

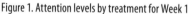

Figure 1. Attention levels by treatment for Week 1

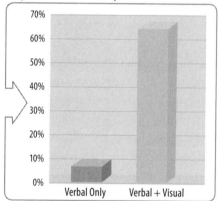

Attention results: test 1. During the first week of testing, levels of attention were remarkably higher when the audience was treated with multisensory communication as opposed to lecture delivery. Specifically, for every one distraction during the multisensory sermons, there were 6.67 during the lecture sermon.

Attention results: test 2. During the second week of testing, levels of attention were not as distinct as the first week of testing. Nonetheless, attention levels were higher when the audience was treated with multisensory communication as opposed to lecture delivery. In particular, for every one distraction during the multisensory sermons, there was 1.4 during the lecture sermon.

Attention results: test 3. During the third week of testing, levels of attention were significantly higher when the audience was treated with multisensory communication as opposed to lecture delivery. For every one distraction during the multisensory sermon, there were 2.5 during the lecture sermon.

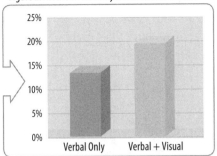

Figure 2. Attention levels by treatment for Week 2

Attention results averaged. The average attention levels for the three weeks of testing demonstrated that multisensory communication consistently outperformed lecture delivery. On average, attention levels were 142 percent higher when the audience was treated with *Verbal + Visual Communication* as opposed to just *Verbal Communication*.

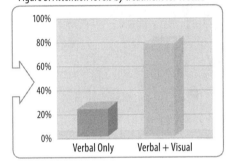

Figure 3. Attention levels by treatment for Week 3

Friend, do not miss these results. My teaching effectiveness in terms of gaining the attention of the audience more than doubled! When I switched from lecture to multisensory communication, my batting average improved significantly. What batter would not love to double his batting average? What salesman would not love to double their sales average?

During these observations, other factors were evident that were not measured. For example, you could see audience posture changes; many people actually sat forward or sat up in response to

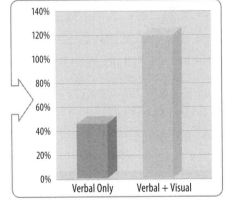

Figure 4. Attention levels by treatment for all tests

the visual and interactive portions. Whereas they had been relaxed, they now demonstrated excitability. Both testing and casual observations demonstrated the superiority of multisensory communication in attracting and holding attention.

COMPREHENSION: MAKING IT TO SECOND BASE

Confusion is so frustrating! How many of us have sat through a lecture at school or church but had no idea what the teacher was seeking to communicate? We walk away from such experiences with no ability to act on what

was taught. Again, our audience will be hard pressed to act on what they do not comprehend.

Therefore, after hooking the attention of the congregation, the teacher must now be concerned with the issue of *comprehension*. If gaining audience attention is making it to first base, second base requires audience comprehension. In my research, I also discovered that effective teachers are experts at clarity. Whether the information is simple or complex, they get it across.

Jesus often brought up the issue of comprehension in his teaching. As noted above, in Mark 7:14 he not only brought up the issue of attention, but he also raised the issue of understanding. "Again Jesus called the crowd to him and said, 'Listen to me, everyone, and *understand* this'" (Mark 7:14, italics added). The Greek word used here is *suniemi*, which denotes "to have an intelligent grasp of something that challenges one's thinking or practice."[13] The idea is taking in information and holding it together so that it makes sense. Many times we teach, but our audience cannot hold it together and make sense of it all. When that happens, the hopes of getting to home plate are dashed.

If Jesus concerned himself with making his teaching understandable, so must we. Granted, understanding is a two-way street between the teacher and the student, but the teacher must make sure that his or her method of teaching is not a roadblock for learning.

Comprehension Is a Brain Matter

Comprehension is a phenomenon that occurs inside the brain. Much more is understood today about that event thanks to modern science and modern technology. Recent advances in neurological surgery, the MRI, and other technological advances have allowed scientists to view the brain as it receives information from the senses.

In fact, scientists are now able to capture the brain *in the very act of learning.* Remember the comic strip analogy of a light bulb coming on in the brain to depict a person who becomes aware of something? It really is a "pattern of light bulbs," according to a study conducted by the Rothman Research at Baycrest Center for Geriatric Care.[14] The study captured the interest of neuroscientists and was touted as a significant contribution to understanding how the brain works when conscious learning is taking place.

Resent research also shows that visual learning increases the activity in our brains. Here is what researchers at the Department of Experimental Psychology, University of Oxford, discovered:

> The ventral prefrontal cortex plays a role in the learning of tasks in which subjects must learn to associate visual cues and responses. Imaging with both positron-emission tomography (PET) and functional magnetic-resonance imaging (MRI) reveals learning increases in activity when normal subjects learn visual associative tasks.[15]

As we will see in the following chapter, some people require visual aids and interactive involvement to make the "light bulbs come on." They comprehend information better if the information is presented in a visual and participatory form.

Test Results

Let me recall the question we were asking in this section: Does multisensory communication outperform lecture communication in terms of *audience comprehension levels*? The results of our test research confirm that it does indeed. The comprehension portion of the test compared audience comprehension levels in three separate tests. In each test, the audience was treated with three kinds of teaching delivery:

Verbal
Verbal + Visual
Verbal + Visual + Interactive

Comprehension results: test 1. During the first week of testing, levels of comprehension were significantly higher when the audience was treated with multisensory communication as opposed to lecture delivery. Stated another way: Levels of comprehension were significantly higher when the audi-

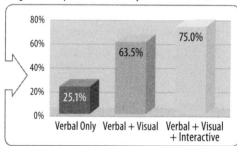

Figure 5. Comprehension levels by treatment for Week 1

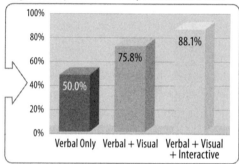

Figure 6. Comprehension levels by treatment for Week 2

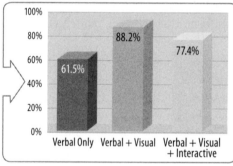

Figure 7. Comprehension levels by treatment for Week 3

ence was treated with *Verbal + Visual Communication* as opposed to just *Verbal Communication*. Levels rose even higher when the audience was treated with *Verbal + Visual + Interactive Communication*.

Comprehension results: test 2. During the second week of testing, levels of comprehension were again significantly higher when the audience was treated with multisensory communication as opposed to lecture delivery. The results confirmed the results of week 1. The more senses we added to the teaching, the higher the comprehension levels.

Comprehension results: test 3. During the third week of testing, the results were identical to the first two weeks. Levels of comprehension were again significantly higher when the audience was treated with multisensory communication as opposed to lecture delivery.

Comprehension results averaged. The average comprehension levels for the three weeks of testing demonstrated that multisensory communication consistently outperformed lecture delivery. On average, attention levels were 76.1 percent higher when the audience was treated with *Verbal + Visual + Interactive Communication* as opposed to just *Verbal Communication*.

What an improvement in my teaching effectiveness! My teaching effectiveness in terms of getting the message across to the audience increased by an average of 73 percent when I added visuals, and by 76.1 percent when I added visuals and interaction. Again, what batter would not love to increase his batting average by 76.1 percent? I am convinced that this kind of clarity has helped me clarify the Word of God and the vision God has for Christ Fellow-

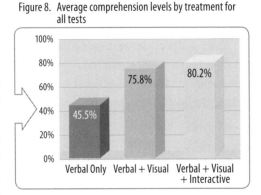

Figure 8. Average comprehension levels by treatment for all tests

ship, and it has helped get our congregation to the home plate of doing God's Word. I am convinced it can help you do the same. Remember, it's not just talent, it's also technique.

RETENTION: ROUNDING THIRD BASE AND HEADING FOR HOME

Memory is crucial to action because people cannot act on what they do not recall. This is why the psalmist said, "I have hidden your word in my heart that I might not sin against you" (Psalm 119:11). The psalmist knew that controlling his sinful nature depended in a large measure on his ability to recall God's Word. Great teachers separate themselves from the pack by communicating in a way that is memorable.

In the spiritual realm, the ability to recall God's Word is what feeds our soul. If those we teach cannot remember the information we teach, it will fail to feed the soul and impact behavior.

Making it Stick

Many cognitive experts are convinced that we can recall more of what we both hear and see, because the data "sticks" like duct tape in our minds. When we add interaction to the mix, memory is increased even more.

Let me recall again the question we were asking in this part of the test: Does multisensory communication outperform lecture communication in terms of *audience retention levels*? Is it true that visual and interactive teaching can make material stick longer in the mind of our audience?

The results of our test research confirm that it does indeed. The retention portion of the research design compared audience retention levels in three separate tests. In each test, the audience was treated with three kinds of teaching delivery. They are:

Verbal Only
Verbal + Visual
Verbal + Visual + Interactive

Retention results: test 1. During the first week of testing, levels of retention were significantly higher when the audience was treated with

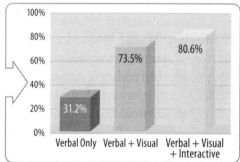
Figure 9. Retention levels by treatment for week 1

multisensory communication as opposed to lecture delivery. Stated another way: Levels of retention were significantly higher when the audience was treated with *Verbal + Visual Communication* as opposed to just *Verbal Communication*. Levels rose even higher with *Verbal + Visual + Interactive Communication.*

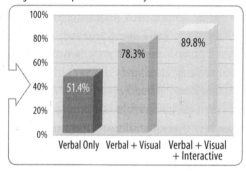
Figure 10. Comprehension levels by treatment for Week 2

Retention results: test 2. Likewise, during the second week of testing, levels of retention were again significantly higher when the audience was treated with multisensory communication as opposed to lecture delivery. Levels rose even higher when the audience was treated with *Verbal + Visual + Interactive Communication.*

Retention results: test 3. During the third week of testing, levels of retention were again significantly higher when the audience was treated with multisensory communication as opposed to lecture delivery. Levels did not rise higher in this treatment when *Interactive Communication* was added to *Verbal + Visual.* Nonetheless, multisensory communication significantly outperformed lecture.

Retention results averaged. The average retention levels for the three weeks of testing demonstrated that multisensory communication consistently outperformed lecture delivery. On average, attention levels were 74.6 percent higher when the audience was treated with *Verbal + Visual + Interactive Communication* as opposed to just *Verbal Communication.*

Again, what a significant improvement in my communication effectiveness! My teaching effectiveness in terms of making the message memorable increased by an average of 62.2 percent when I added visuals and by 74.6

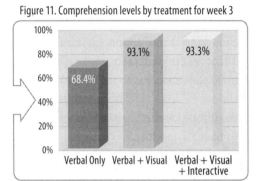

Figure 11. Comprehension levels by treatment for week 3

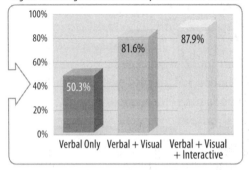

Figure 12. Average retention levels by treatment for all tests

percent when I added visuals and interaction. Again, what batter would not love to increase his batting average by 74.6 percent?

A Fascinating Result

There was a fascinating development that occurred in the retention testing. As I have already indicated, the sermons were preached over a period of three weeks. The retention test was then given at the end of the last sermon of the third week.

You might expect people to remember more about the message of the third week because they took the test immediately after hearing it. You would also expect them to remember less about the message of the first week insofar as they were three weeks removed from that sermon.

But that was not always the case. For example, if they were exposed to multisensory communication on week 1 and lecture communication on week 3, they actually had better recall of the information from week 1 than week 3. In other words, they remembered more about the multisensory message even though they were three weeks removed from it (73 percent accuracy) than about the lecture message they just heard (68 percent accuracy). Why? It's because the information was visually and interactively etched into the minds of the audience. They had heard it, seen it, and participated in it, and that translates into long-term memory.

AVERAGING ALL THE RESULTS

When we tallied up the results for the tests on comprehension and retention, my average improvement with multisensory communication was 75.3 percent.

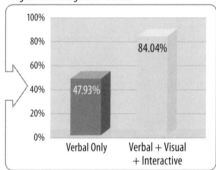

Figure 13. Average of all Results

Depending on where people are as communicators, multisensory communication will move good teachers to great teachers and great teachers to phenomenal teachers. This is also enough of an improvement to have a significant impact on audience action, and we have seen it at Christ Fellowship. It has shown up in the growth of our church, both spiritually and numerically.

By the way, we have spread the "multisensory love" to our entire church. From the toddlers, to the children, to the youth, to the adults, our church has become a multisensory learning experience. Christ Fellowship raised and spent close to two million dollars to transform traditional lecture classes into highly visual and interactive learning environments. The difference has been extraordinary. Parents tell us that their children and youth beg to come to church.

Finally, multisensory communication is not only the buzz around our church, but it is also becoming the buzz in our community. Unsaved people show up at our church to see the multisensory teaching that takes place from the children to the adults. It has helped us grow as a church, and I truly believe it can help you in the same way.

For me, it's like playing golf. Golf is about 30 percent talent and 70 percent technique. Great communication is similar. If you could raise the level of your communication by these levels, would you make the investment to change your communication style? Let's talk about it.

DISCUSSION QUESTIONS

1. As you prepare your teaching, do you think about the outcome? Do you say to yourself, "This is what I want the people *to do*"?

2. As you prepare to teach, do you think about the learning process?
   - Do you think about gaining attention?
   - Do you think about being crystal clear?
   - Do you think abut being memorable?

3. Which part of your communication would you like to work on most? Why?
   - Gaining attention
   - Being more clear
   - Being more memorable

4. If you make the change to multisensory communication, which will be the easiest for you to implement: visuals or interaction?

EYEWITNESS:
THE NEUROLOGICAL PROOF

*The strong man is the one who is able to intercept at will
the communication between the senses and the mind.*

NAPOLEON BONAPARTE

I'll never forget the first color television my dad purchased. Finally, we were going to see television programs in living color. To help us receive broadcast signals, Dad purchased a high-powered multiangle antenna. It rotated in a complete 360-degree circle, which gave it the capacity to receive multiple channels. At that time, there were basically three networks on the air: ABC, NBC, and CBS. In other words, Hollywood had the capacity to communicate through three networks, and our multiangle antenna gave us the capacity to receive all three.

Unfortunately, even with this high-powered antenna, we received only one channel clearly — NBC. Why only one channel? The answer was simple: ABC did not broadcast any signal to Rock Hill, South Carolina, and CBS did not broadcast a clear signal.

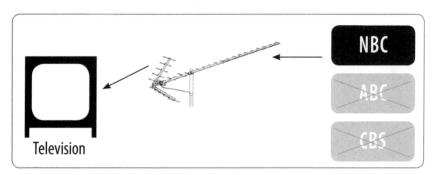

Television

On the receiving end, our TV was wired to receive all three channels: ABC, NBC, and CBS. But only one channel communicated to our television — NBC. The communication breakdown was not on the receiving end. It was on the communicating end.

This is the picture of much modern-day preaching. The breakdown in communication is often on the teacher's end. As biblical teachers, we have three sensory channels by which to communicate information — verbal, visual, and interactive. Corresponding to that three-dimensional communication, the people in our congregation have a three-channel neurological antenna by which to receive that information. They can *hear* the verbal communication, they can *see* the visuals, and they can *touch* the interactive elements.

But in most churches, the information is broadcast in one channel only — verbal. Most pastors are "verbal only" communicators. In other words, if you don't learn well by hearing, you are out of luck. Bear in mind that most pastors are not insensitive. It's just that they have been taught to teach in one dimension only. For visual learners, that one-dimensional style of teaching looks like this:

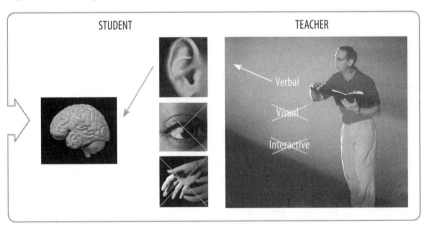

To finish my story, shortly after my parents got our color television, ABC and CBS finally began to broadcast to the Rock Hill area. Suddenly we were receiving signals from all three channels, and we loved it.

At Christ Fellowship Church, we try to communicate from all three channels (verbal, visual, and interactive) to the corresponding senses of reception (hearing, seeing, and touching).

EDUCATORS R US

For those who serve as pastors, we must remember that we have a dual role. We are *leaders* and *teachers*. That dual role is bound up in the job title

Scripture gives to us: *pastor-teachers* (Ephesians 4:11). As *pastor*, we must be competent shepherd-leaders of the flock over which the Holy Spirit has placed us. In fact, the spiritual health and the numerical growth of the church are largely dependent on competent leadership from the pastors. To address that need, books on pastoral leadership are being written in a seemingly endless chain.

But I must add: *Competent teaching* is just as crucial to the spiritual health and numerical growth of the church. We will be hard-pressed to grow our churches if we struggle to communicate the things of God's Word. Therefore, we must not forget the other half of our calling, which is to teach. In fact, 1 Timothy 3:2 says the pastor must be "able to teach." The phrase "able to teach" is a translation of the Greek word *didaktikos*, which means "skillful at teaching."

The work of skillful teaching carries us onto the two-way street between the teacher and the learner. Skillful teaching requires the transfer of information from the mind of the teacher to the mind of the learner. It is in that transfer that learning happens or fails to happen.

Multisensory teachers are strategic in this transfer process and aim directly at the senses of the student. They do not, of course, go only for the senses. Rather, they aim at the senses as the gateway into the mind. They understand that only by going through the gate of the sensory receptors can the mind be accessed.

Senses: Gateway to the Brain

As educators, we might think learning begins with the brain. But this is not the case. Learning occurs within the brain and information is processed there, but learning does not *begin* there. Learning begins with the senses. This is precisely why the senses cannot be ignored when it comes to sound biblical teaching. The senses are not some ancillary afterthought of teaching and learning. Rather, the senses initiate learning; they are the gates to the brain. What follows may get a little technical, but we need to understand the physiological-neurological role of the senses as it relates to the cognitive science of learning.

The five senses receive information from the environment and transmit that information to the brain for processing.[1] Williams compares the senses to an antenna on a television. Barbee and Swassing compare the sensory system to channels or modes through which an individual receives and retains information.[2] With either analogy, the point is the same: The senses function like receptors from the environment. When it comes to communication, people receive sensory information from the teacher in the form of hearing, seeing, and touching and then transmit that sensory information to the brain for processing. According to Mark Grabe of the University of North Dakota, "Intellectual perception involves the recognition of information collected from the environment by the sensory receptors."[3] In other words, all learning begins by receiving information from the environment through the senses.

Senses: Avenues to the World

I need to take us on a journey into the anatomy of the brain and the transfer of information from the senses to the brain. In his text *The Biochemistry of Memory*, Dr. Samuel Bogoch observes the role of the senses in learning: "Sensory transduction is the process by which the information from the environment, received by specialized peripheral sensory receptors, is converted to the language of the nerve cell for transmission, abstraction, storage, and other operations of the central nervous system."[4]

Bogoch's point is that the neurological chemistry between the senses and the brain determines the *reception* function and the *retention* function. Put another way: The conduit between the senses and the brain determine attention levels, comprehension levels, and retention levels. This means that the senses are indeed the gate to the brain — to its attention, comprehension, and retention. As a result, if we as teachers wish to maximize learning levels, we must deliberately aim our communication at as many senses as possible.

Later in his book, Bogoch laments that the science of sensory reception has been almost completely ignored by educators. In other words, educators tend to ignore the influence of the senses when it comes to learning and memory. Among many evangelicals, teaching that aims at the senses has been demonized — seen as worldly, fleshly, and nothing more than entertainment.

Bogoch, however, provides several good reasons for paying attention to this aspect of molecular events. "First, this is the *initial event* in the chronology of *reception* and *recording* of information by the nervous system. Second is the fact of chemical coding for experiential information, which is largely if not entirely accomplished at the *input end* in the process of sensory transduction."[5] Or, as Richard Lazarus puts it, "our senses are our 'avenues to the world.' The only way we have of responding to the outside world is on the basis of information received, and operated on, by our sensory systems. This fact puts sensory psychology in a unique place in the history of science."[6]

Let me spell it out as clearly as possible: Cognitive learning in the brain is initiated at the input end, which are the senses. Lynn Hamilton, in her landmark work on autism, says this about the brain and the senses: "Without one's senses, the brain would be like an eternal prisoner locked within the confines of one's skull."[7]

Toward a Theology of the Senses

The role of the senses in learning is not only supported by neurology but also by theology. Three primary senses interface with teaching: *hearing*, *seeing*, and *touching*. Scripture recognizes each of these sensory receptors in 1 John, where the apostle John writes: "That which was from the beginning, which we have *heard*, which we have *seen* with our eyes, which we have looked at and our hands have *touched*" (1 John 1:1, italics added).

Note the three channels through which individuals learn: (1) hearing, (2) seeing, (3) touching. The subject of the text is Jesus, "that which was from the beginning." John's point is that he and the others learned from Jesus by *hearing* him, by *seeing* him, and by *touching* him with their hands. As far back as 1933, A. T. Robertson understood this: "Three senses are here appealed to (hearing, sight, touch)."[8]

Hebrews 5:14 also makes the connection between the senses and the transfer of information to the brain. "But strong meat belongeth to them that are of full age, even those who by reason of use have their senses exercised to discern both good and evil" (KJV). The senses are seen in this text as a vehicle for helping the mind to discern good from evil. The word "senses" here is a translation of the Greek word *aistheterion*, which means "sensory perception" and "intellectual understanding."[9] This entry goes on to comment: "The *aistheteria* [senses] are the organs which are capable of, or at least susceptible to, discrimination between good and evil, the τέλειος having trained them by exercise."[10]

INDIVIDUALS IN YOUR AUDIENCE HAVE SENSORY PREFERENCES

Not only do preachers and teachers need to be aware that the senses are the gateway to the brain, but also they need to know that everyone in their audience has a sensory preference. Everyone has a dominant sense that is his or her optimum sense for learning. An understanding of these prefaces and sensitivity to them is the key to multisensory communication.

Auditory learners. Many of the people who sit in our congregations and classrooms do not need visuals to learn nor do they need to interact

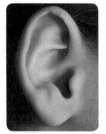

directly with the teacher. For the auditory learner, it is enough for the teacher to communicate with verbal clarity. In fact, this learner prefers to learn and learns best through the sense of listening. He or she is concerned with the logical flow of information and comprehends and understands best when the information is auditory.

Such auditory learners learn best through verbal lectures, discussions, talking things through, and listening to what others have to say. Some people are so proficient at learning through the hearing channel that incoming information that is not auditory may actually interfere with their learning. For example, if a speaker is referring to charts and graphic illustrations, this learner may need to ignore that part of the presentation (even closing his or her eyes) in order to focus on the auditory information.[11]

At Christ Fellowship, I have had a few occasions when the message was perhaps overly visual or overly interactive, and this type of learner expressed some difficulty with paying attention and comprehending the message. Such cases have made me more sensitive not to overkill with visuals and interactive aids.

Visual learners. This individual learns best through seeing the material or concept being taught. He or she may struggle to understand and

remember the information unless it can be seen. Needless to say, the eyes are an intrinsic part of the learning process for all of us who have the gift of sight. Many scientists believe seeing is the dominant sense for most people. "One of the most important problems in sensory psychology is the specification of the stimuli we study. Visual stimuli come from a narrow band in the electromagnetic spectrum, a band that covers wavelengths of radiation ranging from 400 millimicrons to 700 millimicrons. From these environmental stimuli the *dominant sense of sight* is stimulated."[12] According to Rudolf Arnheim, professor of the psychology of art at Harvard University, "practically all thinking — even theoretical and abstract — is *visual* in nature."[13]

Our eyes are truly sensory wonders. Because of these two jelly-filled spheres, we are able to perceive incoming information in terms of size, shape, color, and location of objects. Our eyes can shift, adjust, and focus on objects as close as the end of our nose and as far away as a distant galaxy. The vast number of receptors in our eyes tells us just how involved the eyes are in the sensory process.

> In the visual system, nerve cells look out at the world through their connections from the one hundred million receptors in each eye. When physiologists turned their recording microelectrodes on these *visual* neurons, the results were a revelation. For each cell seemed ... to be *searching for meaningful combinations of features*, for the boundaries and shapes in the image that define the edges of objects.[14]

For persons whose dominant sense is vision, they learn most effectively when information is visually presented or at least visually aided. As a matter of fact, for some the sense of vision is so dominant that they are forced to compensate if the communication is nonvisual. Ulrich observes, "If the visual way of learning is particularly strong for you, you may often try to picture in your mind what you are learning. You may even be accused of daydreaming or being lost in thought."[15]

Interactive learners. These individuals learn best through moving, doing, and touching. They are referred to as tactile/kinesthetic learners,  and they have a desire to explore the physical world around them. They may find it hard to sit still for long periods. Interactive learners need to touch, handle, and do something with the information being taught. For example, if they were being taught the mechanics of typing, they need the keyboard to actually do some typing.

Aircraft pilots know about this kind of learning. Their auditory learning comes through listening to flight instructors and reading flight instruction books. Their interactive learning comes through actually flying the plane or through the flight simulator. Lectures may be helpful, but pilots will tell you they really learned how to fly the plane when they put their hands to the steering and instruments.[16]

Peter Kline points out, "You were born to learn with your whole body and all your senses. You were not born to sit in a chair eight hours a day and listen to someone talk, or to pour over books year in and year out."[17] Willis and Hodson affirm the same concept: "The traditional school model not only shortchanges interactive learners, it also shortchanges all the other learners, because lessons that incorporate moving and doing are helpful for everyone."[18]

To sum up, an individual's dominant modality is the sensory channel through which information is processed most efficiently. Traditional education has often ignored learning preferences through which a student maximizes learning and accelerates learning rates. John MacArthur recognizes the importance of learning preferences when he writes:

> How do you learn best? Preferences vary from person to person. For some people the best way to learn a new concept or digest new information is simply to sit down and carefully read through pages of printed material. For others it's sufficient to take notes as someone else describes a process or explains a fresh idea. But for some of us the best way to thoroughly grasp an idea is to *participate* in it or be an *eyewitness* to a practical application of the principle.[19]

MacArthur recognizes the different ways in which people prefer to learn and in which they learn best. He also acknowledges that people have sensory preferences for receiving information. Some people learn best through hearing, others learn best when the information is presented in a visually rich form, while some need to participate in the learning. The fact that people have different sensory preferences for learning is the reason for multisensory communication.

UNDERSTANDING BRAIN HEMISPHERE DOMINANCE

Furthermore, it is not just sensory *preference*; in most cases it is sensory *dominance*. Neurological and cognitive research clearly demonstrates that individuals have a dominant sense — that is, a dominant channel through which they best receive information.

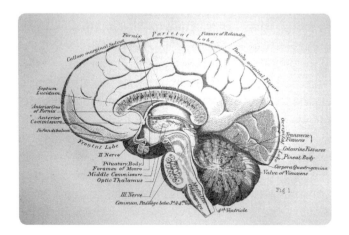

Tucked inside each of our heads is a three-pound jellylike mound that resembles crinkled Play Dough. It is actually a connection of over one hundred billion neurons. As scientists have continued to probe inside this neurological wonder, they have discovered that the brain is actually a two-hemisphere entity. They have also discovered that each hemisphere is unique from the other in terms of function and concentration. The two halves are generally referred to as right brain and left brain.[20]

Both hemispheres process information received from the senses, and most people tend to be stronger on one side than they are on the other. Many cognitive scientists believe that *sensory dominance* is determined by *brain hemisphere dominance*. The conclusion of many researchers is that the left-brain dominant person is strong in verbal learning, while the right brain dominant person is strong in visual learning.

Interestingly, brain hemisphere dominance tends to fluctuate throughout a person's life, but typically the pattern is determined in childhood. Researchers say your eyes and other body signs indicate the pattern of switching hemispheres. For example, one may observe that some people fold their arms in different ways — left over right or vice versa. Trying to change the way one folds the arms will quickly demonstrate how comfortable that person is with the way he or she has learned to do it, and any other way feels strange.[21] This fact indicates one's pattern of hemispheric dominance at the time a person learns to fold his or her arms. For most of us, this occurs between ages two and three. The feeling of strangeness when we try to change the pattern demonstrates how comfortable we have become with the initial choice we made and how infrequently we have challenged that choice.

An understanding of brain hemispheres becomes essential to teaching and preaching strategies when we understand that brain hemisphere dominance may be responsible for certain learning preferences. In the context of teaching, the left-brain dominant learner can learn easily through a lecture format and probably learns best through a lecture format. The left side of their brain is the dominant side, so they process information without the need of visual or tactical involvement. Most teaching institutions, grade schools, colleges, and churches cater to their learning style, insofar as most teaching institutions teach in a lecture-only format.[22]

The right-brain dominant learner is attracted to the visual side of learning. This person typically needs to see information to grasp it and retain it in short- and long-term memory. Because the right side of the brain is the dominant hemisphere, seeing becomes the dominant sense for receiving information. Unfortunately for this kind of learner, most of our teaching institutions, including the church, are auditory and monosensory in delivery methodology.

In his classic work *Teaching for Results*, Findley Edge has written, "Learning must start where the student is."[23] However, because many educators do not understand the concept of student learning styles, teaching does not begin where the student is, but where the teacher is.

"WHAT WE HAVE HERE IS A FAILURE TO COMMUNICATE"

Those are the infamous words uttered by Paul Newman in the movie *Cool Hand Luke*. They have since become a catchphrase referring to what happens when communication breaks down between the communicator and the person being communicated to. It is also an apt description of what happens between pastors and congregations. Often there is a failure in communication on the part of pastor and a consequential failure in learning on the part of the congregation. This is tragic and unnecessary, because unless there are neurological-physiological problems, the brain has great capacity to learn. That learning capacity can be helped or hindered by the teaching style of the teacher.

One of America's leading psychologists and educational experts, Paul Witty, relates a story about an educational encounter he experienced with an elementary school child. He had worked with the child for several hours, but to his frustration, the child was not learning the task Witty was seeking to impart. In exasperation, he said to the child, "What's wrong with you?" Without a moment's hesitation the child blurted back to him, "What's wrong with *me*? What's wrong with *you*? *You* are what's wrong!"[24]

Learning is a two-way street between the teacher and the pupil. Sometimes the roadblock in the learning process is in the lane of the teacher. Sometimes, we are "what's wrong." "If students have difficulty learning the way we teach, perhaps we should teach the way they learn."[25]

MATCH YOUR TEACHING STYLE TO ALL LEARNING STYLES

The *learning styles theory* implies that how much individuals learn has more to do with whether the educational experience is geared toward their particular *style of learning* than whether or not they are *smart*. In fact, educators should not ask, "*Is* this student smart?" Rather, they should ask, "*How* is this student smart? Is the student *hearing smart, visually smart,* or *interactively smart*?"

When it comes to teaching the Word of God to our congregation, we must ask the same question: How are these people smart? In our congregations, there are all three kinds of *smart*. In a congregation of six hundred, there may be two hundred who are hearing smart, two hundred who are visually smart, and two hundred who are interactively smart. Unfortunately, most preaching and teaching is geared only to the hearing smart. That must change!

Research to understanding the connection between teaching style and learning style began in the mid-1970s. In 1976, G. Pask wrote an article in *The British Journal of Educational Psychology* in which he hypothesized that maximum learning capacity could be increased when the teaching style of the teacher matches the learning style of the student.[26] Subsequent to his article, experiments were conducted matching teaching styles with student learning styles, and the experiments have confirmed his hypothesis.[27]

As pastors with educational objectives, we must not turn a deaf ear to the matter of learning styles and teaching styles. Note what John MacArthur writes:

> If someone would have asked the apostle Peter what *learning style* he preferred, he might well have said that the up-close, hands-on style was his favorite. That certainly would have fit his character as an action-oriented man of initiative. As his mentor and Lord, Christ knew exactly how best to convey the truth to Peter's heart and mind. *And as the perfect teacher,* Jesus wisely involved him directly and indirectly, in His miracles, parables and sermons.[28]

Jesus did not embrace a one-size-fits-all teaching methodology. He clearly adjusted his teaching style to fit Peter's learning style. As an educator, Jesus was ahead of his time in terms of teaching strategy and cognitive understanding. He used multisensory communication to get his message across.

PASTOR-TEACHERS: BE AWARE OF YOUR PERSONAL SENSORY BIAS

Research has demonstrated that the teacher's own personal sensory preference tends to influence the method and style by which he or she teaches. Barbee and Swassing warn that teachers tend to project their own learning preference into their selection of materials, teaching strategies, procedures, and methods of reinforcement. In other words, we tend to teach as we learn best, not how the students learn best:

Consider, for instance, the primary grade teacher who is highly audi-tory. The natural tendency of this teacher is to stress phonics as the best and perhaps the only way to attack new words. The method worked for the teacher when he or she was learning to read and provides the teacher with an opportunity to organize a lesson around his or her area of strength. As the teacher expected, most of the class (those who were auditory or auditory in combination with one of the other modalities) learned the skills associated with the phonics method. The remainder of the class had more difficulty using phonics to learn new words, but the teacher continues to hope that with more practice, they will learn appropriate word attack skills.[29]

In other words, teachers must be aware of a sensory bias because they will tend to teach in a style that matches their learning preferences.[30] Pazmiño concurs: "The greater challenge is to incorporate a variety of styles or to teach in one's dominant style, while allowing for a degree of flexibility to accommodate the learning styles that are generally repre-sented in any group of learners."[31]

In research conducted by Nater and Rollins, they found an alarming statistic about learning preferences. They looked at 1,500 adults who had dropped out of school in the eighth grade and found that 99.60 percent of them were sensing-dominant learners. In other words, they were visual and interactive learners. Next, they interviewed 671 adults who were final-ists for National Merit Scholarships. Using the Myers-Briggs Type Indi-cator they found that 83.01 percent of the scholarship individuals were intuitive type learners.[32]

This research demonstrates that in our educational institutions, those who learn primarily through the senses (i.e., visual and interactive learn-ers) are penalized while those who are intuitive learners are rewarded by the very way in which they are taught and tested. Multisensory teach-ing will leave no learner out. It will enable you to connect to your entire audience.

A CLOSING NOTE TO THE LAYPERSON

Dear layperson reading this book: If your pastor is seeking to teach in a multisensory form, please don't complain that *you* don't need it. Recall that others who are visual and interactive learners desperately need multisen-sory communication in order to grasp the truths of God's Word. Remem-ber the words of John MacArthur, "How do you learn best? Preferences vary from person to person." Remember too, it is not all about you!

DISCUSSION QUESTIONS

1. What kind of learning style do you prefer?
    *   Hearing
    *   Hearing + visual
    *   Hearing + visual + interaction

2. What is your teaching style?
    *   Verbal
    *   Verbal + visual
    *   Verbal + visual + interaction

3. Has your learning style influenced your teaching style? If so, how?

4. Are any learners being left out in your classroom or congregation?

CHAPTER 5

EMBRACE:
THE THEOLOGICAL ENDORSEMENT

The Word of God is the universal and invisible light, cognizable by the senses, that emits its blaze in the sun, moon, and other stars.

ALBERT PIKE

There is a heated debate going on in evangelical churches about the use of multisensory preaching. Sides have been taken and theological swords have been drawn. In this brief chapter, we simply want to be biblically sensible. The goal is to answer three questions raised with regard to multisensory preaching.

1. Does the Bible forbid the use of multisensory teaching?
2. Does multisensory teaching "water down" the gospel message?
3. Is multisensory teaching simply entertainment?

The first question has to do with *permission*. Do we have biblical permission to teach in a multisensory form, or is it prohibited? The second question has to do with *purity*. Does multisensory preaching compromise the purity of the text? The third question has to do with *objectives*. Does multisensory preaching seek merely to amuse the audience?

DOES THE BIBLE FORBID THE USE OF MULTISENSORY TEACHING?

For me, if the Bible forbids multisensory communication, it must be abandoned at once. If the use of visuals, props, media, drama, and other multisensory teaching aids somehow violate a biblical command or principle, I will be the first to reject it. But if there is no such prohibition and if there is actually biblical precedence for this model of communication, then let's embrace it fully.

Multisensory Objections

Let me say at the outset that those who object are well-intentioned and often wonderful teachers of the Word. I have no desire to be offensive, only to state the case of those who object and to evaluate their statements biblically.

One evangelical who has been outspoken against multisensory communication is Arthur Hunt. He suggests that multisensory teaching "dumbs down the church" and leads us in the path of pagans. He contrasts our Judeo-Christian heritage, which he states is "word dependent," with paganism, which he claims is "image dependent." He warns that by exalting visual imagery we risk becoming mindless pagans, and that we are open to abuse by those who exploit image but neglect the Word.[1]

Another outspoken dissenter of technology and multisensory teaching gives this rather lengthy complaint:

> As technology has continued to advance, pictures have become more prominent and words less so. This should be a great cause of concern for Christians. It is difficult to communicate a word-based religion to an image-oriented society. Alarmingly, rather than leading the culture, the church has succumbed to this trend. Worship services in many churches have become mindless. The Word of God has been dumbed down. Focus and reading and exposition of the Word have been replaced by entertainment such as monologue jokes, dramatic presentations, and even dance performances. This has resulted in congregants seeking little importance in learning or knowing God's Word or teaching the Word of God to the next generation. This opens the door for the rise of paganism and, as Hunt contends, the rule not by the Word-based Constitution but by a dictator who is able to rise through creating an acceptable campaign image.[2]

This seems incredible! The author implicitly links the use of multisensory teaching to the rise of the Antichrist! He calls vision-oriented teaching "mindless" because he fails to realize that the eyes and other senses are conduits to the brain. Visual communication does not seek to bypass the mind; it simply seeks to reach the mind through the mental receptors, that is, the senses. What he also fails to recognize is that people learn in different ways.

John MacArthur takes a similar position, appearing to view any kind of preaching other than lecture as compromising the Word. He complains:

> Some will maintain that if biblical principles are presented, the medium doesn't matter. That is nonsense. If an entertaining medium is the key

to winning people, why not go all out? Why not have a real carnival? A tattooed acrobat on a high wire could juggle chain saws and shout Bible verses while a trick dog is balanced on his head. That would draw a crowd. And the content of the message would still be biblical. It's a bizarre scenario, but one that illustrates the median can cheapen the message.[3]

This author makes a major leap from multisensory preaching to a "real carnival with a tattooed acrobat on a high wire juggling a chain saw and shouting Bible verses." Should we accuse Jeremiah, Hosea, and Jesus of conducting "a real carnival"? Is using a visual like an ox yoke being "circus like"? Is using a harlot for an illustration over the top? Is pulling a coin out of the mouth of a fish being too dramatic? Andy Stanley offers some wise advice to those who use multisensory elements in their teaching of the Word:

This brings us to an important reason for careful planning: ensuring that the message of the Bible is the central focus of the weekend services. Visuals can be illuminating. Videos can move and inspire. Lights and props and drama can keep people interested. But too much of a good thing can quickly distract from the very reason people need to be there, which is to apply the Word of God to their lives.[4]

God Is a Multisensory Communicator

Thumb through the pages of the Old Testament, and you will quickly discover that God is into multisensory communication. In fact, he is the pioneer of multisensory communication. God designed us with multiple senses to receive information from the environment, and he constantly seeks to connect to those sensory receptors.

Multisensory natural revelation. God teaches us about himself from what we hear, see, touch, smell, and taste. This is what theologians refer to as *natural revelation*, because God is revealing himself and teaching us through what we sense from nature. The multisensory nature of the creation captivates our attention, helps clarify our understanding of God, and is absolutely unforgettable. Edwin Hubble said, "Equipped with five senses, man explores the universe around him and calls the adventure science."[5] God gave us this amazing universe; he communicates the universe through sound, vision, feel, smell, and taste; and he gave us the five corresponding senses to perceive it.

Multisensory special revelation. God also teaches us in a multisensory form when it comes to *special revelation*, that is, the Bible. Throughout the

Old Testament, God taught theological and practical truths though multisensory communication. His sensory teachings were graphic, explicit, and directly connected to the truth he wanted to communicate.

For example, God often called on his prophets to use extreme multisensory teaching methodologies in order to connect to the audience what he wished to impart. They used verbal communication mixed with visual elements as well as interactive techniques to heighten the levels of attention, understanding, and memory of the people.

Hosea: Drama ahead of its time. For those of you who imagine drama is an unscriptural form of teaching, you must read the book of Hosea. Here God is the teacher, and to make the lesson stick, he used a real-life drama. God himself set up this real life multisensory sermon by having Hosea marry an adulterous woman.

GOD'S VISUAL TEACHING

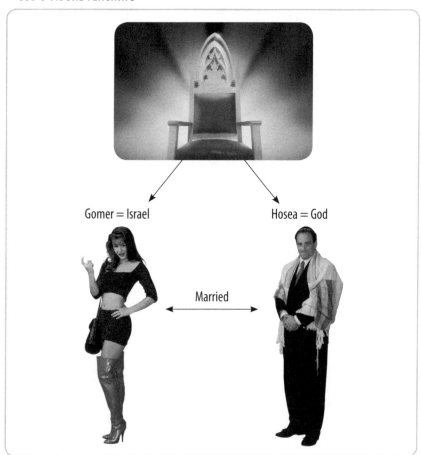

"When the LORD began to speak through Hosea, the LORD said to him, 'Go take to yourself an adulterous wife and children of unfaithfulness, because the land is guilty of the vilest adultery in departing from the LORD'" (Hosea 1:2). The adulterous prostitute, whose name was Gomer, represented the spiritual adultery committed by Israel against God. By marrying an adulterous woman, Hosea was giving a visual picture of Israel's spiritual adultery. Every time Israel looked at the relationship between Hosea and Gomer, they saw a multisensory sermon of their own adulterous relationship with God.

Jeremiah: Video ahead of its time. God called Jeremiah to carry an ox yoke on the nape of his neck, and the image spoke to the people as graphically as possible. Calvin Miller writes, "This image was video ahead of its time."[6] God was using Jeremiah as a walking three-dimensional visual object lesson to teach Israel a truth.

One can find other multisensory teaching examples in the Bible from God. The entire tabernacle, set up as prescribed by God, was a visual picture of worship in heaven. The Passover drama played out in Egypt pictured the blood of the Lamb of God on the cross. The pastor who teaches in a multisensory form is not mimicking the culture; he is mimicking the Creator.

Jesus: A multisensory teacher. Few teachers relied on the power of multisensory teaching more than Jesus. What we are seeing today in terms of multisensory teaching is not so much a *revolution* as it is a *revival*. Jesus used vines, branches, coins, water, wheat, wheatfields, children, and all sorts of visual aids to graphically communicate divine truth. Roy Zuck discusses the teaching methods of Jesus:

How did Jesus engage such attention? His teaching competence is seen in his creative use of variation in teaching patterns, the way he involved his learners, and his appeal to the visual. Teachers today do well to learn from Jesus' teaching by stimulating and motivating their students, varying their methods, encouraging learners to participate, and visualizing what they verbalize.[7]

New Testament Ordinances Are Multisensory

The ordinance of baptism paints a visual picture of a theological reality. We even remind our congregations that baptism is a *picture* of the death, burial, and resurrection of our Lord Jesus. A picture paints a thousand words, and baptism does just that. It is an explicit image of a great theological truth.

The Lord's Supper is even more multisensory. The bread is a picture of Christ's body, and the juice is a picture of his blood. But it's more than just verbal and visual; it is also interactive. The congregation interacts with the teaching by eating the bread and drinking the juice. In addition, there is the stimulation of the senses of taste and possibly smell. The Lord's Supper is the ultimate form of multisensory teaching, because it interfaces with all five of our senses: hearing, seeing, touching, tasting, and maybe even smelling. Talk about graphic!

The answer to Question 1: We have permission to use multisensory preaching. There may be preachers and teachers who decide not to use this means, and that is fine. I am not saying this is for everyone. But come to your senses and do not make it a biblical-theological issue. There is theological precedence for those who wish to make use of its effect.

QUESTION 2: DOES MULTISENSORY TEACHING WATER DOWN THE GOSPEL MESSAGE?

When some evangelicals accuse modern-day preaching of watering down the gospel, I concur with them. Many contemporary churches have put the church on a slippery slope of compromising the purity of the biblical text. John MacArthur accuses them of "watering down" the gospel message, and in some cases he is right.

This is tragic, because when a preacher waters down the message, he strips the octane out of the message. He is robbing the message of the fuel it needs to ignite changed lives. But not all multisensory preaching falls into that category. In fact, there are some who teach in a purely lecture format who water down the message. Style is not the issue, content is.

Fired Up — Not Watered Down

Multisensory communication, when executed with loyalty to the biblical text, has the opposite impact of watering down the message; if anything, it makes the truths of the Word more explicit. It makes them visual, graphic, and unforgettable. Multisensory communication does for preaching what symbolic language does for the book of Revelation. Such symbolic language is not allegory; it is literal truth made more graphic by the language. That's precisely what multisensory communication can do for our preaching. It adds special effects to the message. These special effects do not water down the communication; rather, they make it more graphic.

The message we teach must never be altered, toned down, or compromised. As Bible teachers, we must resist the temptation to preach in a form that is palatable and acceptable to all. Again, much seeker-driven preaching jettisons the theologies of judgment and wrath from the teaching and makes all preaching "happy talk."

The Bible is not all "happy talk." God warns of judgment and eternal death. We must not reject preaching that warns people of eternal separation from God. Don't get me wrong: I see some pastors who seem to relish the idea that people are going to hell. They speak of it as if they enjoy the thought. We must not go there either. Let's speak the truth and communicate it graphically, but let's do so with compassion and love.

Changeable Methods

Multisensory preaching by nature does not seek to change the message, only the method of delivery. It is designed to make the message more captivating, more understandable, and more memorable. The communication world is constantly in change, and we must be able to adapt our methods (not the message) to that context. The world of communication has transitioned from no technology to radio, television, computers, and the Internet. The church itself has transitioned from no PA systems to microphones and to high-tech sound systems. We have evolved from no means of recording messages to reel-to-reel tapes, cassette tapes, CDs, DVDs, and now podcasting. Through many of those changes, there were dissenting voices that accused them of being evil and of the devil. It's sad that the church does so much to make itself ineffective.

The answer to Question 2: Multisensory teaching does not water down the gospel.

QUESTION 3: IS MULTISENSORY TEACHING SIMPLY ENTERTAINMENT?

Some fundamentalists view the pulpit itself as a doctrinal issue. Any form of teaching that replaces the pulpit as a means of communicating the Word is seen as compromising and as theological error. One well-known advocate of lecture only preaching complains that "instead of a pulpit, the focus is a stage."[8] The suggestion seems to be that only pulpit teaching is pure and any other method of teaching is deemed to be "entertainment." This same person goes on: "There seems almost no limit to what modern church leaders will do to entice people who aren't interested in worship and preaching. Too many have bought the notion that the church must win the people by offering them alternative entertainment."[9]

What Does "Entertainment" Mean?

The implication is that any form of teaching other than lecture falls into the realm of entertainment. That criticism, however, raises a question: Exactly what is entertainment, and is entertaining teaching an unpardonable sin for teachers? Webster defines "entertainment" as "something engaging." Is that not our goal as teachers of the Word, to engage our parishioners' minds intellectually? The word "entertain" is also defined as "to keep, hold, or maintain in the mind." Is that not our mission as communicators of the Scriptures? Are we not trying to keep, hold, and maintain in the mind the Word of God?

I am struggling to understand the complaint. I am having a hard time finding a theological problem with that kind of teaching. Do we not wish to engage people's minds? Do we not wish for people to hold and keep what we are teaching in mind? In fact, when I check the antonym of "entertain" on my computer, I get the word "bore." Are we trying to bore our people, or are we trying to captivate their minds so we can impart truth?

If we were talking about grandstanding and trying to amuse people, I too am against that. I admit I have seen some multisensory teaching that was carnival-like. I loathe that as much as any lover of the Word. That, however, is not my understanding of entertaining the mind of an audience. Hosea was attempting to use multisensory teaching to entertain and engage the minds of the Israelites.

I Plead Guilty

Calvin Miller makes a revealing contrast between "entertainment" and "interest." "Entertainment and interest pass very close. It's difficult to tell if a sermon has interested or entertained the audience." He continues by saying, "In some sense then, I believe that all can experiment with how to hold an audiences attention. To entertain means to occupy time engagingly. Every time I am prone to doubt the value of this engagement, I turn again to the arts for the best demonstration of this. Movies, plays, novels, and paintings all have the same glorious virtue: the arts intrigue us as they teach us."[10]

The answer to Question 3: Multisensory teaching is entertaining in the sense that it engages the mind.

There is a story in the epilogue of this book that I want you to read. Please do not forget to do so.

DISCUSSION QUESTIONS

1. Are there any direct prohibitions in the Bible that forbid the use of multisensory teaching methods?

2. What effect do you think Hosea's message had on the people? How would you have related to his visual message?

3. What would you think if your pastor or teacher showed up to teach with an ox yoke tied around his or her neck?

4. What effect does the Lord's Supper have on you as you see the bread and juice and as you physically participate in its lesson?

5. Did you see the movie *The Passion of the Christ*? If so, what effect did it have on you?

CHAPTER 6

EXPERIENCE:
THE POWER OF BIBLE EXPOSITION AND
MULTISENSORY COMMUNICATION

I do feel obliged to believe that the same God who endowed us with sense, reason, and intellect has not intended us to forgo their use.

GALILEO

The United States space shuttle vehicle has the power to break the bonds of gravity and carry human beings on sense-sational journeys. To achieve that power, NASA engineers have married two powerful forces together: main engines and solid rocket boosters.

As the 120-ton vehicle sits on the pad, surrounded by almost four million pounds of rocket fuel, exhaling noxious fumes, it seems visibly impatient to begin its journey. At precisely t-minus 6.6 seconds, if the pressure, pumps, and temperature are "go," the onboard computers give the command to light the shuttle's main engines. At that moment each of the three engines ignite precisely 160 milliseconds apart, and the engines ramp up incredible amounts of energy. As the engines come to one million pounds of thrust, their exhaust tightens into blue diamond flames. But it is not yet time to release the beast. The shuttle is held in its place yet for a few more seconds.

Then, at t-minus zero seconds, if the computers are satisfied that the main engines are running at full power, they give the order to ignite the solid rocket boosters. In less than one second, they reach 6.6 million pounds of thrust! Then and only then do the computers give the order for the explosive bolts to blow, and the 4.5-million-pound shuttle lifts off the launching pad and the sense-sational journey begins.

The combination of the shuttle's main rocket engines and the solid rocket boosters creates vast amounts of energy. In only two minutes the shuttle achieves a speed of three thousand miles per hour. In less than six and a half minutes it will accelerate to 17,500 miles per hour — the speed needed to achieve earth's orbit.[1]

THE POWER OF BIBLE EXPOSITION

What a picture of multisensory Bible teaching! The Word of God must always be the main engine of our teaching. It is the force that carries the power of God himself. Adding multisensory communication to our preaching, however, is like adding the solid rocket boosters to the space shuttle. The combination of biblical content and multisensory communication can boost our teaching to indescribable dimensions.

Biblical Engine + Multisensory Booster = Phenomenal Power

Paul gave this charge to Timothy: "In the presence of God and of Christ Jesus, who will judge the living and the dead, and in view of his appearance and his kingdom, I give you this charge: *Preach the Word*" (2 Timothy 4:1 – 2a, italics added). Paul inserts a great amount of intimidation in that charge. He calls on God and Christ Jesus as his witnesses, and then, with those two members of the Godhead present, he gives this charge to every pastor: "Preach the Word." Paul also gives an outline of the preaching process: "Till I come, give attendance to *reading*, to *exhortation*, to *doctrine*" (1 Timothy 4:13, KJV, italics added). There is a three-part sequence to this injunction: The pastor-teacher is to (1) read the text, (2) explain the text, and (3) apply the text. This is a great definition of expository preaching.

It is his Word that God has promised to bless. "So is my word that goes out of my mouth: It will not return to me empty, but will accomplish what I desire and achieve the purpose for which I sent it" (Isaiah 55:11). The ministry of the Word in the church is not secondary to the church's success; it is the very core of it.

Don't Abandon the Core

In spite of God's promise to bless his Word and in spite of the command to "preach it," some contemporary pastors have made a conscious decision to jettison biblical preaching from the pulpit. Noted professor of biblical exegesis Walter C. Kaiser marks this trend, which pervades so many evangelical churches. "It is no secret that Christ's church is not at all in good health in many places in the world. She has been languishing because she has been fed junk foods, all kinds of artificial preservatives, and all sorts of unnatural substitutes have been served up to her."[2]

It seems odd to me, but among many contemporary pastors, there is almost a disdain for Bible exposition. Just as there is a disdain for multi-sensory preaching among many expositors, there is disdain for exposition among contemporary teachers. I don't get either one! In some circles, when I say that I am an expository preacher, I get this *look* that makes me think I have said a curse word. Some contemporary pastors view verse-by-verse Bible exposition as out of touch and ineffective. My fear is that we are abandoning who we are at our very core.

If I preach the Bible verse-by verse, will it somehow weaken my sermons? If I follow the logical flow of God's writing, will my message be illogical? Is God's Word, as written, out of touch with mainstream society? If I teach it in its historical and grammatical context, will it not relate to the needs and hurts of people I am speaking to?

W. A. Criswell is a great man who used Bible exposition to reach multitudes of people. To say exposition of Scripture is impotent to reach the lost is nonsense. As far back as 1742, John Albert Bengal offered this challenge to the church regarding its fidelity and commitment to the Scriptures: "Scripture is the foundation of the Church and the Church is the guardian of the Scripture. When the Church is in strong health, the light of Scripture shines bright; when the Church is sick, Scripture is corroded by neglect."[3]

Many pastors give lip service to the power and authority of God's Word, but they relegate it to second class when it comes to their preaching. John MacArthur shines the light on this: "Evangelical preaching ought to reflect our conviction that God's Word is infallible and inerrant. Too often it does not. In fact there is a discernable trend in contemporary evangelicalism away from biblical preaching."[4]

Anti-Intellectual Preaching

There also appears to be a prevailing wind of "anti-intellectualism" among many contemporary preachers. This mindset insinuates that the people in our audiences do not have the intellectual capacity to comprehend mentally challenging content. As a result, some contemporary pastors tone down the theological and cognitive content of their teaching. I heard one popular speaker say he keeps his content on a seventh-grade level. He was applauded.

The problem with this approach is that it limits the theological growth of our audiences and thereby limits their relationship with God. Beyond that, it implies to the world that Christians lack the capacity to think, reason, and engage in mentally stimulating thought. Christianity then comes across as a simplistic, mindless, emotional, and nonintellectual faith.

THINGS ARE A-CHANGING

One well-known contemporary pastor says of unchurched people, "They like Jesus, but not the church." He then cites some qualities that unchurched people would like to see in a church. One of those qualities is: "I wish they would respect my intelligence." He also quotes an unchurched individual who went to church and described the experience as, "I felt like I was at a Tony Robbins seminar with a couple of Bible verses thrown in."[5]

This pastor has nailed a major disconnect between the modern church and the lost. Non-Christians tend to believe Christians are afraid to engage in critical thinking. They imagine we have our heads "in the sand" in terms of logic, science, and even theology. And much of the so-called "teaching" in our churches only reinforces their presuppositions. Much of contemporary teaching is a mile wide and an inch deep, and it lacks maturity. When the lost come in among us and witness such shallow and juvenile teaching, they laugh.

Many contemporary pastors think the world imagines Christianity to be "irrelevant." I don't think that is the problem. I think they imagine Christianity as naïve, and much of the teaching serves to reinforce their belief. As I talk to young non-Christians (those in their twenties), they are offended by juvenile preaching. It is an insult to their intelligence! This is purely anecdotal, but many tell me that the church is devoid of mentally stimulating information. One young man told me that his generation is weary of sermons that are, as he put it: "Ten Ways to Overcome Guilt"; "Twelve Ways to be Happy"; "Twelve Ways to Improve your Sex Life." Another person said: "When I come to church, I feel like unscrewing my head and placing it beneath the seat, because nothing will affect me from the head up."

It is true. In some churches, preaching and teaching seems more like an Alcoholics Anonymous program. The twelve-step template is simply laid across all human maladies with a Scripture text added to make it feel scriptural. Contemporary preaching is all-too-often shallow, it lacks the substance of Scripture, it fails to engage the mind, and it is laughable. This will not build the church or reach the unchurched.

Thom Rainer asserts that such thinking is simply one of the many myths held by some "church growth experts":

> Myth #6: We must be careful in our preaching and teaching so that we do not communicate deep and complex biblical truths that will confuse the unchurched. "You know what frustrated me the most when I started visiting churches?" Susan M. asked us. Susan was a lifelong unchurched person living in the Cleveland area until a crisis prompted her to seek God. She tried to find him and his truth in the churches she visited. "What really frustrated me was that I had a deep desire to understand the Bible, to hear in-depth preaching and teaching," she continued. "But most of the preaching was so watered-down that it was insulting to my intelligence."[6]

I am afraid that many pastors today imagine themselves to be on the cutting edge, but in reality, they are not. They are still preaching in an adolescent form that worked five years ago, but that will not work with rising generations. Content matters to this emerging generation. Let's not fool ourselves into thinking lost people are simple-minded — they are not. Whether they are saved or lost, people do not wish to be talked to in a way that comes across as childlike.

We must step up our game. We must teach the complex things of Scripture as well as the simple truths. By mixing biblical content with multisensory communication, I am convinced everyone will "get it."

THE PERFECT MARRIAGE

The multisensory effect is validated by the Bible, by science, and by the testing presented in this work. This method of delivery stands on its own, and yet there are those who wish to demonize it. I don't get it. We have two powerful forces that need to be married: the Word of God and multisensory communication.

For me, it's not only like the space shuttle combination; connecting exposition and multisensory communication is also like a marriage made in heaven. Unfortunately, there are people on both sides of the theological aisle who are determined to prevent such a marriage from occurring. They both dislike each other for reasons that are unbiblical.

It Doesn't Have to Be "Either-Or"

We have those who love exposition rejecting multisensory communication, and we have those who love multisensory communication rejecting the power of exposition. There is the pervasive feeling that you either have to be one or the other, but not both. You can be an expository teacher but not multisensory. Or, you can be a multisensory teacher but not expositional. What a shame that we hamstring our effectiveness with such unbiblical legalism on both sides. Let's connect these two God-given forces so that we can be more effective for the kingdom's sake.

What's Next?

You have been introduced to the multisensory revolution. You have learned how an audience responds to multisensory communication. You have seen the evidence of its effect from the disciplines of neurology, theology, and research experiments. You have sat in the congregation, as it were, and witnessed the side-by-side effects of multisensory communication versus lecture. The evidence is in, and it cannot be ignored.

Now it is time to get specific and practical. In Part 2, you will be guided through the "how to" portion of this book. We will wrestle specifically with how to use multisensory communication to gain attention, communicate with clarity, and make it unforgettable to your audience. It is now time to become a multisensory teacher.

DISCUSSION QUESTIONS

1. Why do we often see in today's church a breach between Bible exposition and multisensory communication?

2. Have you ever witnessed a serious exposition of the Word presented in a multisensory form? Describe it. Did it work? Did anything not work?

3. What help will you need in terms of being able to marry exposition to multisensory communication?

PREPARING A MULTISENSORY MESSAGE

To me the mind seems to be spread out in the whole body — the senses are part of the brain.

SHARON OLDS

Jim Collins, in his book *Good to Great*, asks some poignant questions about the capacity of a company to elevate its quality status. "Can a good company become a great company, and if so, how?"[1] We are seeking to answer that question as it pertains to our teaching quality. Can a good teacher become a great teacher? And can a great communicator become a phenomenal communicator — and if so, how?

Part 1 of this book answers the "can" question: Can multisensory communication improve your teaching?" Yes indeed! Part 2 now moves into the "how" question: How can you design messages that are multisensory? We now shift to the brass tacks of making it a reality.

Few people comprehend the pressure that Bible teachers face each week, especially pastor-teachers. The pressure of coming up with new messages that are informative, compelling, clear, and memorable is unimaginable. When you add to that the stress of caring for a flock of people, it is a wonder anyone survives. I personally have known pastors who have quit the ministry simply because they could not keep up with the pressure. They felt it would be better to quit rather than resort to teaching that was status quo.

The average person sitting in our congregation, unfortunately, has no idea of the blood, sweat, and tears it takes to deliver messages at such a high level week after week. The weekends come at us like the tides of the ocean. They are nonstop, and as soon as one weekend is over, the clock is already ticking for the next. Yikes, it makes me edgy just writing about it! My prayer continues to be that this book will help lighten your load while elevating the level of your teaching impact.

You are highly honored! God has chosen you, called you, and anointed *you* to teach his precious Word. Granted, you could do something easier with your life, but you could not do anything more significant! In spite of the pressures and disappointments of preaching and teaching, there is no higher calling. Paul said, "I thank Christ Jesus our Lord, who has given me strength, that he considered me faithful, appointing me to his service" (1 Tim. 1:12).

In light of the fact that God considers you to be faithful, be the best teacher you can be for him. For God's sake, take the skills you have been given and make them great! Make them phenomenal! That is the objective of the following chapters. The goal is to make your teaching compelling, clear, and unforgettable. You are on the path to phenomenal Bible teaching.

From the proceeding research, the following formula emerges as a guide to phenomenal Bible communication:

Verbal Communication + Visuals + Interaction = Maximum Impact

The concept is simple. The more senses we stimulate in the learning process, the higher the levels of learning. By adding the additional senses of seeing, touching, and interaction to the communication process, we add high octane to our teaching impact.

Part 2 of this book will be loaded with practical instruction for becoming a high-octane, multisensory teacher. This section will also be peppered with multisensory sermon ideas and multisensory techniques that can be easily used by the reader. Please feel free to use any and all sermon materials presented in this book. If you are like me, you probably can use all the ideas you can get your hands on.

One final thing: Most of the ideas and examples come from my own personal illustrations and examples. You can find other examples that are perhaps better, but I am offering my own for reasons of integrity. I do not wish to use the work of other pastors and teachers without their permission. I hope you will see from my examples that you can pull this off. Whether you teach in a small context or a large context, it makes no difference. You can do this.

CHAPTER 7

PREPARATION:
GET READY FOR MULTISENSORY JOURNEYS

That which was from the beginning, which we have heard, which we have seen with our eyes, which we have looked at and our hands have touched — this we proclaim concerning the Word of life.

JOHN (1 JOHN 1:1)

N ASA rockets carry humans on spectacular journeys. Such journeys enable them to experience the wonders of the universe in a way that is compelling, clear, and unforgettable.

Great Bible teachers do the same for their audience. They carry the people into the universe of God's Word. As a Bible teacher, every time you open the Word to teach, you have the potential to take your congregation on a journey that is compelling, informative, and unforgettable. Multisensory sermons literally make the journeys *sense-sational*.

LAUNCH PREPARATIONS

Just as there are preparations needed for a space shuttle launch, there are preparations needed for the launch of a new methodology of Bible communication. To implement a multisensory form of teaching in your church, you must prepare yourself, and you must prepare your audience for the changes that lie ahead. Such preparation can prevent a disaster.

Relax: This Is Not Going to Be Complicated

My goal is to help make you a phenomenal communicator without making your life more cluttered and complicated. For those readers who are church leaders, I know the burdens you bear, the pressures you face, and the time constraints on your life. I face them as well. The last thing you need is something that demands more work and more of your time.

For that reason, you should know that becoming a multisensory teacher will not complicate your life. You will be able to deliver compelling and unforgettable sermons in a form that is simple and uncomplicated. You can make your multisensory communication more sophisticated as resources grow. Initially, however, this will be simple to prepare and execute.

Have you ever gone to a seminar, taken notes, come home all excited, and were ready to make changes? Then you suddenly realized you didn't have time to make it happen. I can relate. The daily responsibilities of the ministry have a way of pushing new ideas onto the back burner. All the materials and notes go on the shelf, and soon it is back to business as usual.

I promise not to do that to you. Multisensory communication is uncomplicated or I would not be able to execute it either. I preach once on Saturday evening, three times on Sunday, and then again Sunday afternoon at another Christ Fellowship campus just south of Miami. That load will increase to two additional campuses by next year. If multisensory teaching were complicated, I would have to abandon it. It is not.

Admittedly, I have managed to assemble a multisensory team to help me. As that team has grown, the complexity of the multisensory components has grown as well. That has not placed an undue burden on me, however, because the multisensory team has assumed much of the burden. They have made it their ministry to make the sermons more and more powerful. We will talk more about how to assemble such a team in the next chapter. You can do it too! When you finish this book, I pray your communication will not be "business as usual," but rather will be "unusual."

Get Pumped: This Is Going to Be Fun

As I write this section, it is Saturday afternoon. In less than two hours, our Saturday evening services will begin. I had to get to the computer to express the thrill I am feeling right now. This is what multisensory teaching has done for me personally. For whatever reason, it fires me up to the point I can't wait to teach the Word!

Let me give you an image of what we are doing at Christ Fellowship this weekend. We are teaching through the gospel of Matthew in our weekend services, and tonight we launch a new series called: "WAR: Defeating Temptation." The series will be a four-part exposition of Matthew 4:1 – 11, which chronicles the temptations of Christ by Satan. Just a casual glance at this narrative, and you immediately know that this was an all-out war.

The war, however, is not restricted to Satan and God; it is also between Satan and us. Whether we like it or not, Satan has declared war against God's people, and we are locked into a struggle against him. His goal is to drag us down into sin, destroy our lives, and destroy our testimony. To accomplish his objectives, he deploys a formidable arsenal of temptations.

Our single-minded goal throughout this series is to get people to realize they are at war. Christians must have a "war mindset" when it comes to fighting temptation or they will lose the battles. To etch that reality into their mind, the church campus has been transformed into a war zone. Christ Fellowship has the appearance of a theater of military operations.

Tonight, greeters and ushers will be dressed in military fatigues. Peppered throughout the campus are objects and images of warfare. The stage has been transformed to resemble a war zone. There are military tents and military weapons, and even a military MASH unit [Mobile Army Surgical Hospital] has been set up on the stage. The MASH unit will be used later to talk about restoring our wounded brothers and sisters who fall into sin.

The sermons will launch with war videos as well as with a cleaned-up version of the 1960s song, "War: What Is It Good For?" To further drive home the truth, Eric Geiger and I will be teaching in military garb. The effect will be instant. People will be drawn into the sermon as soon as they walk onto the campus. The whole campus screams WAR!

I trust you are getting the point. This is thrilling! Just like you, I love to teach God's Word. In addition, I love to communicate it in a form that is engaging, crystal clear, and unforgettable. But the pressure to deliver messages that are compelling is stressful, and after a while, that stress can zap the joy out of our calling. We can act pious and pretend we are exempt from that pressure, but the reality is, the human casualties of ministry highlight the pressures.

Multisensory teaching can breathe new life into your calling. It can bring a sense of thrill and expectation to your teaching. Stated another way: Multisensory communication can help make your teaching *fascinating* for your audience and *fun* for you. Picture it: Tonight, I am excited, our multisensory team is pumped, and our people have a sense of expectation when they see such explicit communication. Simply put, I am having the time of my life! So can you.

PREPARE FOR A SENSE-SATIONAL CHANGE

Change requires *preparation.* Changing from lecture communication to multisensory communication is no different. As the teacher, you will need to prepare in three dimensions: (1) yourself, (2) your audience, and (3) your teams.

As the teacher, the manner in which you deliver your teaching will change. *Content* will not be changed, but *delivery methodology* will. That change may seem weird at first; it may feel awkward; it may even feel wrong. You will need to be prepared for that change so that it does not mess with your head. I must admit, when I first started teaching with multisensory aids, it felt weird and awkward. Quickly, however, it felt natural. Just as *a lecture teacher* feels most natural behind a lectern, you will soon feel most comfortable beside your teaching aids.

For your audience, the manner in which they *receive* the teaching will change. Be aware: Just as flocks of sheep can panic over change, spiritual flocks have a tendency to panic and overreact to change. You will need to shepherd them through the change so they are not upset by it. If you are in a new church start, this may not apply to your situation. If you're in an established church, don't skip over a planned transition time.

Team work. Although you can produce and deliver multisensory messages by yourself, I highly recommend that you assemble a team to assist you in the effort. I will guide you through that process. It is not rocket science.

The key to preparing yourself for this change is to transition at a pace that best suits you. Don't attempt to make radical changes without giving yourself time to learn the ropes. Here are some simple guidelines to help you successfully navigate the change.

1. Start Simple

This is a major rule for beginning a new style of teaching. Don't start with complicated multisensory elements. Start out simple. Begin your transition from lecture to multisensory with a few object lessons as well as some simple interactive tools. Doing it this way can pay huge dividends in terms of gaining attention, establishing clarity, and creating long-term memory.

I began the move to multisensory communication by introducing my messages with simple teaching aids in my hand. For example, I would walk to the platform with props such as:

- A child by the hand
- An FBI agent with me
- Tire iron
- Golf club
- Laptop
- Boxing gloves
- Bobsled
- Fire hose
- Bottled water
- Pumpkin
- Shovel
- Basketball
- Fishing rod
- Bicycle
- Salt
- Magnet
- Trumpet
- My daughter

These were simple beginnings for me, but they allowed me to get used to the new method.

2. Keep It Manageable

One of the keys to effective multisensory teaching is smooth management of the props and interactive tools you are using. It has to seem *effortless* and *seamless*. The key to a "effortless and seamless feel" is being able to manage your props and tools. Trying out a new teaching method can make you feel self-conscious. Just keeping up with your emotions at such a time is enough, much less trying to manage something complicated. If you are struggling to manage multisensory teaching tools, it will be distracting to you and distracting to your audience.

Shortly after using simple multisensory aids, I attempted some fairly complicated stuff, and I was not ready. As a result, the teaching was difficult to manage. It seemed clumsy, awkward, and unnatural. No one said anything to me, but I knew it was awkward. My congregation is forgiving, and I think they knew I was trying hard.

You should start simply and keep it manageable. Increase the complexity as *you* adjust, as *your congregation* adjusts, and as *your human resources* grow. In part 3 of this book, we will present different levels of multisensory teachings. They will range from simple, to intermediate, to complex. The key is to advance the complexity at a rate you can manage.

3. Embrace Your Strengths; Avoid Your Weaknesses

Just as you have verbal communication strengths, you will also have multisensory strengths. My personal strength is the use of props and interactive tools. When I have props in my hand and tools that engage the participation of the audience, I feel as if I have an assistant teacher with me. Sometimes, I almost feel as if I am cheating, because it makes the teaching so easy to execute. Props and interactive tools help me grab attention, create intellectual clarity, and instill long term memory. I feel comfortable with them.

I struggle, however, with the use of drama. I have been able to implement visual art with great success, but I have struggled to use dramatic arts. I recognize that drama is one of the most powerful forms of communicating a point. If you have never watched Andy Stanley use drama in his sermons, you have missed a treat. He is a master. Drama can grab your attention, impact your emotions, and make a theological point like few other forms of communication can.

Having said that, I personally struggle to make it work. For one thing, you have to have great actors, and Stanley does. Our culture is used to watching A-rated actors on television. If we use B-rated actors ill equipped for such a presentation, it can come across as cheesy. I have not given up on drama, but I realize my limitations. Don't force it if you don't feel ready for it.

4. Keep Learning and Developing

One factor I love about teaching the Bible is that it is a lifetime learning experience. To keep our communication style fresh and captivating, we must have two non-negotiable traits:

- teachable spirit
- a willingness to learn from others who are different from us

Many pastors and teachers develop one style of communication at the outset of their ministry and then never tweak it. As a result, they become predictable to their audience, and after a while they tend to sound like a broken record. Be honest: How predictable do you think your teaching is? Is it fresh each week, or can the audience put their mind on autopilot?

5. Learn from a Variety of Teaching Styles

Sometimes pastors and teachers become prideful about their teaching method and eventually become unteachable. They may attend conferences to improve their teaching, but it is always the same style. The result is a teaching rut. I see two extremes among evangelical pastors and teachers. The fundamentalists seem narrow-minded and the contemporaries seem simple-minded.

Narrow-minded fundamentalists tend to emphasize Scripture exposition and deemphasize communication strategies. For them, exegesis seems to be the single-minded goal. As a result of that narrow-minded goal, they learn only from those who seek to advance exposition.

Simple-minded contemporaries tend to pursue the reverse. Communication techniques are emphasized to the neglect of an intellectual consideration of the text. In many such messages, the Bible is used as a springboard to launch a series or a sermon. Exegetical accuracy is sometimes a nonissue. The single-minded goal in such teaching is attention, and such teachers are unwilling to learn from those who advance exposition.

In other words, many contemporary teachers tend to succeed at homiletics while failing at hermeneutics. They are unconcerned with this as long as they communicate to people's lives. Expositors, by contrast, tend to succeed at hermeneutics while failing at homiletics. For them, it is okay to miss the communication connection so long as you get the interpretation right.

On both sides of the ledger, there is failure. One side communicates but gets the information wrong. The other side gets the information correct but doesn't get it across. We must be proficient in both disciplines.

This week, I will be traveling to a multisensory communication conference in the Midwest. Although I will not agree with everything, I know I will take away information that will make me a better Bible communicator. My fundamentalist friends will probably think I have compromised by learning from these people.

Last year I attended a conference on exposition. The strategies for teaching emphasized the power of the Word and reinforced my confidence in God's Word. But my contemporary pastor friends thought I was regressing.

The truth is simple: I have a great passion to teach God's Word in the most compelling, most understandable, and most unforgettable way. To do so, I must be willing to learn from both extremes. I don't attend a conference on multisensory preaching and then abandon my commitment to Scripture. Nor do I attend a Bible exposition conference and jettison my commitment to multisensory communication. I mix the two for a powerful, two-punch combination.

Unfortunately, we all tend to be close-minded to anything other than the style that fits the camp we hang out with. Last week, I met with a group of contemporary pastors who gathered to discuss teaching techniques. During the course of the conversation, they were condemning of in-depth teaching that emphasizes the text and theology. They mocked such teachers as being stuck in the past. But they were shocked when I suggested that they may be the ones stuck in the past. I warned them that the church growth landscape that characterized the past decade may be changing and changing quickly. Content and intellect now matter!

To sum up, I have enjoyed learning from both sides. I may read from one person who can make me a better Bible teacher, and I may learn from another who may make me a better communicator. Don't let people force you into one dimension.

PREPARE YOUR CHURCH AUDIENCE FOR THE CHANGE

Who can forget the Challenger spacecraft disaster? The catastrophic explosion and subsequent loss of life and vehicle was the result of two basic mistakes:

- rush to launch
- failure to recognize climate conditions

How many pastors create church disasters simply because they rush to make changes without considering the climate of the church? Again, if you are in a new church start, you will not have to deal with the issue of transitioning your church to a new style of Bible teaching. If, however, you are in an established church, read the following two thoughts carefully. They can help you successfully navigate the change.

1. Transition, Transition, Transition

The culture of your church should determine how you proceed with multisensory teaching. Most of us have plenty enough to deal with without starting a conflict over our preaching and teaching style. For that reason, I encourage you to *transition* your teaching style. People tend to resist drastic change, but they can be led through change if they are transitioned.

To make *teaching style changes* without causing a war, begin with simple multisensory components, not overpowering multisensory ones. Begin your transition with some simple object lessons. It will give you time to learn the ropes, and it will give your congregation time to adjust to the change.

When I became the pastor of Christ Fellowship (then First Baptist Church of Perrine), we were faced with making a host of changes. Not only was the music and structure of the church traditional, even the platform was traditional. It reflected a "lecture only" style of delivery. The platform stage boasted a large pulpit, pastors' chairs, modesty rails, organ, organ pipes, curtains over the baptistery, robed choir, stained-glass window, pews ... you get the picture.

This was in no way a church conducive to multisensory experience. My desire was to transition us to a church that put less emphasis on traditional icons and more emphasis on the communication of the Word. The challenge was daunting. I would need to shepherd the congregation to view the campus, the auditorium, and the stage in new ways.

The key to our successful change was *transition*. By making gradual changes, we were able to create a room that was less concerned with a traditional experience and more focused on an educational experience. These days, when you walk into the auditoriums of Christ Fellowship, it is clear that we are all about teaching and worship. Huge high-definition screens, high-tech lighting, high-tech sound, multisensory images, uncluttered platform, and a stage that is designed for multisensory communication dominate the rooms.

That same communication emphasis is reflected in our children's worship areas and those of the youth and singles. Christ Fellowship is all about communicating the Word. In time, you can transition yourself, your audience, and your campus to a teaching haven.

2. Determine to Keep It Biblical

By keeping your sermon laced with biblical authority, you will keep your sheep at ease. Spiritual sheep seem willing to adjust to methodological change as long as the message hasn't changed. Our teaching needs to be captivating and relevant, but when it lacks solid biblical content, it weakens the flock and can make them restless. Furthermore, from time to time I suggest that you reference God's multisensory teaching methods as well as those of Jesus and the prophets. This will lend biblical authority to the change.

PREPARE YOUR TEAMS

NASA has been able to send human beings on incredible journeys. The

most amazing was the journey to the moon. It truly was "one giant leap for mankind." The capacity to take such journeys, however, resides in human and technical resources. Without both of those, such spectacular journeys would never occur.

You are about to take people on spectacular biblical journeys. Your audience will hear, see, and interact with you as you guide them into the wonders of the biblical universe. To make such journeys, you should gather human and technical resources.

Now, I recognize that it will take some effort to assemble such teams, but once they are assembled, your teaching load will actually be lightened. Bear in mind, you can generate your people teams and technical resources at the pace you expand your teaching. NASA did not begin by going to the moon. They began by simply getting a man into orbit. But as NASA expanded the vision, they required many creative minds and more technical resources.

That is an apt picture of how to proceed. Don't begin by trying to take your audience to the moon. Start small and dream as big as God would have you. Personally, I am still expanding the horizons of my teaching, and I love it. This is part of what makes it so much fun!

The great value of human resources is the deposit of creative ideas and the skills to implement those ideas. *Creative ideas* have to do with the designing of multisensory sermons and sermon series. *Implementation* has to do with the manpower necessary for executing those ideas. Therefore, it is good to divide your human resource team into three separate teams.

- *Teaching team*: teacher(s) who brainstorm and generate the content of sermons and sermon series
- *Design team*: those who brainstorm and design multisensory effects
- *Implementation team*: those who build the multisensory props and settings as well as those who carry them out

TEACHING TEAM: UNLEASHING CONTENT IDEAS

Sermon content must always flow from the heart of the ones God has called to teach. Nevertheless, a "teaching team" can serve as a great advantage for the pastors and teachers who teach week after week. Instead of one brain attempting to come up with all the ideas, you now have multiple brains.

At Christ Fellowship, we have a teaching team, which is comprised of four gifted men called by God to be pastors and teachers. Once a month we gather for a time of brainstorming about upcoming series and sermons. The combining of our pastoral, teaching, and creative minds generates remarkable ideas.

If you have multiple pastors in your church, let me suggest that you assemble a team and tap their creative minds. Also, if you have retired pastors in your congregation (if they have creative minds), they can be advantageous. Even if you carry the teaching load alone, you can still bring them together for a brainstorming session.

Let me give you an example of how we operate. This week, we are planning for our fall series, which will flow from "The Lord's Prayer" in Matthew 6. We are currently teaching through the gospel of Mathew, and we will reach the Lord's Prayer just in time to kick off the fall with this series. The goal of this series is to focus on the simplicity of that prayer. It is a model of simple, uncomplicated, and uncluttered prayer. That is what we want our congregation to take away from the series.

The teaching team brainstormed and came up with this title for the series: "iPray." I love it, and I would never have come up with such a great title on my own. The title captures *the iPhone fascination* of our culture, and it will enable us to guide the audience into the text of Scripture. The factor that makes the iPhone so fascinating is its simplicity. Many cell phones are cluttered with buttons and dials that are complicated to operate and confusing to use. The iPhone, however, is the antithesis of clutter — simple to understand and simple to operate.

That is the exact image that we want to communicate about prayer. Many books on prayer present a complicated maze of things that you are supposed to do in order to pray. In contrast, Jesus gave us a model of prayer that is *iPhone-like*: simple, uncluttered, and easy to follow. That's the content we want to teach.

From there, our Design Team has gone to work on creating a stage setting that will be dominated by the image of an iPhone. For the duration of the series, that giant iPhone will shout about the simplicity of talking to God.

Let me cite another example of teacher brainstorming. Recently, we met to discuss the implications of the life of John the Baptist as recorded in Matthew 11. One of the remarkable statements in that text is that Jesus said John was the greatest man who ever lived. That became the Big Idea that we wanted to drive throughout the teaching of this series.

As we thought about it, I came up with the idea to call the series "The Greatest Life." Something about the title, however, seemed bland — too generic. As we continued to brainstorm, the idea surfaced about the "dash" between birth and death dates, i.e., 1966 – 2046. John's "dash" between his birth and death was the greatest "dash" possible. From there, the simple idea of "DASH" immerged, and a series of six messages was developed. I can't wait to get started!

- Your Dash Will Have Periods of Doubt   11:1 – 11
- Your Dash Should Be Aggressive   11:12 – 15
- Your Dash Will Be Criticized   11:16 – 19
- For Your Dash to Matter — Be a Friend to Sinners 11:19
- Your Dash Will Be Examined   11:20 – 24
- Your Dash and Your Death Matters to Jesus   14:13

DESIGN TEAM: UNLEASHING MULTISENSORY IDEAS

As teachers, it is our calling to generate the sermon *content*. To transform that sermon series into a multisensory learning experience, however, may require other talents. This is where a "design team" can be helpful.

By gathering a team of people with gifts of visual design, your sermons can elevate from good to phenomenal. A design team can take your word content and transform it into a multisensory experience. People with skills to create stage designs, stage props, graphic designs, screen designs, artwork, sculpting, series logos, series titles, and so on will make your sermons graphic. These teams come alongside your content ideas and help you dream up ideas that can make the message more multisensory.

If you decide to gather such teams, prepare for a surge of excitement. There are probably people in your church who are just waiting to use the creative, artistic, and construction talents God has given to them. In some churches, such talents go untapped and even unwanted. What a shame! When I send word that I need help with my sermons, most people feel honored and appreciated to be enlisted on my team.

Several years ago, Eric Geiger and I taught a series of messages on the attributes of God. The series was simply entitled: "What is God Like?" and considered six major attributes of God: (1) God's mercy, (2) God's judgment, (3) God's compassion, (4) God's jealousy, (5) God's wisdom, and (6) God's holiness. During each worship service, as the people sang, an artist painted a visual work of art that matched the particular attribute to be taught. The canvas on which they painted was seven feet by five feet and was easily visible to the entire congregation. These paintings were connected to make the message unforgettable (see appendix B for images of the paintings).

The paintings also presented a visual point of focus as I taught on that attribute. At the conclusion of the series, each of the paintings was connected to make a point that was unforgettable. People are still talking about it. Enlisting those artists to elevate the worship and teaching made them feel as if their gifts and talents were needed and wanted.

Put out the word that you want to assemble such a team: "Calling all artists, builders, graphic designers, fabric designers, interior designers, sculptors, and dreamers." Meet with those who respond and tell them of your vision to create sermons that are captivating, clear, and unforgettable. Share the research from part 1 of this book. Many of them will be well aware of the impact of multisensory communication. They will be excited that you wish to tap their gifts to teach the Word and reach people for Christ.

Let them know as well how valuable they are. There is rarely a week at Christ Fellowship that people are not saved. In our creative meetings, we always review the previous week and remind our teams that they are an invaluable part of the decisions that have been made for Christ.

As you assemble your human resource teams, gather them based on *design* and *implementation*. Initially, one group may carry out both functions, but separate them as soon as possible. This will allow for focus.

IMPLEMENTATION TEAMS: MAKING IT HAPPEN

The "implementation team" is the team that actually takes the creative ideas off the drawing board and makes them a three-dimensional reality. These are the people who create a campus theme around the sermon series, build sets, create works of art, execute the drama, work in media and IT, and so on. When I turn them loose, I am always amazed at their creative ability.

This can get complicated. Grow the explicitness of your multisensory messages only as these teams grow. There is one crucial ability you must cultivate: the ability to recruit volunteers to your teaching vision. You can do this by recruiting not to a *need* but to the *vision* of reaching the lost with powerful teaching. People do not generally respond to need, but they will respond to vision. You will have to sell them on the vision of assisting you in the greatest mission in the world.

As you think of assembling your team, here are some talents you may want to consider:

- Graphic arts
- Floral design
- Construction
- Printing
- Sculpting
- Photography
- Fabrics and textures
- Holiday decorations
- Art and paint
- Media and screens

Depending on how sophisticated you get, you may need some financial support to pull off your sermons. Our people have come to expect creative teaching, so attaining the financing is not a problem. I have managed to build it into my budget. I suggest you start small and build your budget as your multisensory sermons grow.

DISCUSSION QUESTIONS

1. What do you think might be your strong point in multisensory teaching? Props, art, or drama? What area comes easier for you and interests you the most?

2. How are you open to ideas that don't necessarily fit your teaching profile?

3. In what ways will you need to prepare your audience for change to multisensory preaching/teaching?

4. Describe what you understand to be the role of a design team.

5. Describe what you understand to be the role of an implementation team.

**CHAPTER
8**

PROCESS:
DESIGNING MULTISENSORY JOURNEYS

*Nothing we use or hear or touch can be expressed in words
that equal what is given by the senses.*

HANNAH ARENDT

It is now time to implement the multisensory sermon both in terms of its
design and its delivery. This section will help you create powerful multisensory sermons week after week. Two ingredients are necessary: (1) the
people to assist you and (2) the process to guide you. In the previous chapter
we examined gathering people to help you. The present chapter discusses
the process to guide you in creating powerful multisensory messages.

The following chart shows the flow of a series design at Christ Fellowship. You can readily see the handoff from the teaching team to the design
team and from the design team to the implementation team.

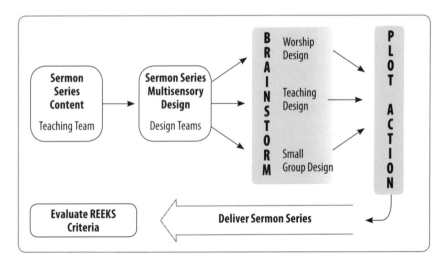

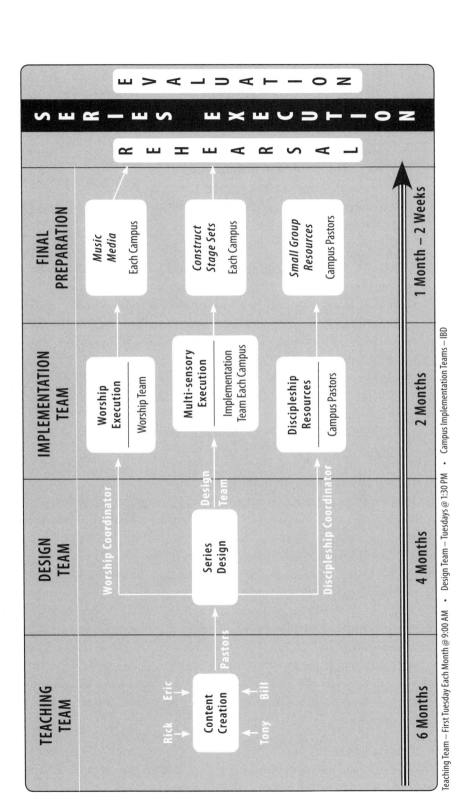

TEACHING TEAM	DESIGN TEAM	IMPLEMENTATION TEAM	FINAL PREPARATION	

S E R I E S   E X E C U T I O N

E V A L U A T I O N

R E H E A R S A L

TEACHING TEAM

Rick   Eric

Content Creation

Tony   Bill

Pastors

DESIGN TEAM

Worship Coordinator

Series Design

Design Team

Discipleship Coordinator

IMPLEMENTATION TEAM

Worship Execution

Worship Team

Multi-sensory Execution

Implementation Team Each Campus

Discipleship Resources

Campus Pastors

FINAL PREPARATION

Music Media

Each Campus

Construct Stage Sets

Each Campus

Small Group Resources

Campus Pastors

6 Months	4 Months	2 Months	1 Month – 2 Weeks

Teaching Team – First Tuesday Each Month @ 9:00 AM • Design Team – Tuesdays @ 1:30 PM • Campus Implementation Teams – IBD

STEP 1: DETERMINE SERMON SERIES

As a pastor, I have found *series preaching* to be the most impactful way to teach the Word of God, especially when the series flows out from a biblical text. A series of sermons announced in advance:

- creates interest
- gives people a reason to invite friends
- provides movement and direction
- generates a sense of audience responsibility to attend each message in the series

By far, our greatest occasions for church growth at Christ Fellowship have been when we have announced a series in advance. Much of the effect came from the fact that a design team made the series theme visually explicit. They worked to etch the theme into the very fabric of the church campus. Series logos, series objects, and series visuals permeated the campus and generated tremendous amounts of interest. I will say more about that work momentarily.

Coming up with the sermon series should be the responsibility of the pastor-teacher or teaching team. As pastor-teachers, God has called us to lead the church, and it is up to us to discern where he is leading. Here are some common-sense tips that may help you as you grapple with the theme of your series.

a. Let It Overflow from Your Quiet Time

For me, everything I teach is the overflow of my quiet time before God. In the early hours of the morning before my family awakens, I get alone before God, and it is there that he impresses in my heart about what I should teach. Even though I generally teach through books of the Bible, it is in my quiet time that God gives me insight into the Big Idea of the sermon series that I extract from his Word.

When I teach courses on preaching and teaching, I always talk first about the need for quiet time. People often ask me, "Where do you get your ideas and illustrations?" Sometimes, there is no rhyme or reason to it. I can only say that in my time alone with God, incredible thoughts pass from his heart into my heart, and I write them down. I always have a pad and pen in my quiet time, because I don't want to miss what God gives me. It works for me; it will work for you.

b. Let It Flow from the Text of Scripture

There is a slogan that is popular among many contemporary pastors: "The *methods* will change, but the *message* will never be changed." I affirm that statement, but in some contemporary churches, it just isn't true. Among some contemporary pastors, the method has changed and so has the message. Simply stated, the message has lost its biblical edge.

I don't want to belabor the point, but I am fearful of the direction that some are leading us in when it comes to preaching. Much contemporary preaching seems devoid of theological content. Pastor-teacher, please don't be afraid to ratchet up the intellectual content of your teaching, and don't be leery of teaching doctrine.

I recently sat in on a conversation with a group of contemporary pastors. They all love the Lord. As they were talking about series preaching, however, I couldn't help but detect a lack of confidence in the Bible. The Bible was not the guiding lamp unto their feet; rather, whatever was popular seemed to be the guide. One pastor mentioned that he was conducting a series entitled "Muppetology" (not the actual title, but close). He was developing "spiritual principles" derived from cartoon characters. I laughed to myself when he said this, because I thought he was joking. He wasn't! He was planning an entire summer series based on *The Muppets*. Please!

Such infantile teaching leads to infantile Christians. We must ask ourselves: Is God so inept at writing his Word that we cannot follow it to teach his people? I continue to hear advice that suggests we cannot teach from the Bible if we expect to reach people with the gospel. Such comments gives critics ammunition to attack contemporary preaching, and rightfully so. I reject the notion that God's Word is useless for teaching on the weekends. It is his Word that God has promised to bless!

Contrary to popular belief, you can teach topically while teaching through a book of the Bible. You do not have to sacrifice relevance while teaching Scripture expositionally. At Christ Fellowship, we have introduced fascinating subjects and developed life-changing series while teaching through books of the Bible. As I have mentioned, we are currently teaching through the book of Matthew, and we are discovering relevant themes as we move though this book. Here is a list of our series that have emerged thus far in Matthew:

Title	Number of Sermons	Matthew Text
Unwrapping Christmas	4	1:1 – 2:24
24: Your Daily Calling	4	3:1 – 12
Baptism: What's it all about? [182 baptisms]	1	3:13 – 16
War: Defeating Temptation	4	4:1 – 11
The Pursuit of Happiness	5	5:1 – 12

Salt and Light	2	5:13 – 14
Myth Busters	4	5:21 – 47
iPray	6	6:1 – 18
Jingle-ology	3	6:19 – 34
Ask God.com	8	7:1 – 28
Move On	4	8:1 – 27
Master-Peace	6	8:28 – 9:38
The Dirty Dozen	6	10:1 – 15
Your " — " [dash]	4	11:1 – 11
REST	4	11:28 – 30
Lose Your Religion	4	12:1 – 50
Parables	6	13:1 – 58
Miracles	4	14:1 – 36

As you can see, topics that are germane to our culture readily emerge from the text of Scripture. We don't have to go on a hunting expedition to find relevant topics; they are resident in the text itself. God's Word is as relevant as a letter tucked in your mailbox, and it is as current as today's newspaper left at your doorstep. Demonstrate to your audience that you really do believe the Bible is relevant in its own right. We have been able to make these series multisensory, and the effect of biblical teaching in a creative format is phenomenal.

c. Look for the Big Idea

As you brainstorm the series theme, think forest, not trees. The *series theme* will be the forest in which the *individual sermons* (trees) reside. Look for the forest first. Some people call this the "Big Idea."

For example, when I examined Matthew 5:21 – 47, there was one "Big Idea" that kept leaping off the page. Jesus was destroying *religious myths* that were pervasive in his day and that are still widespread in our day. A religious myth is essentially a man-made religious teaching that has no biblical counterpart. The Pharisees were notorious for spreading religious myths. There are at least four religious myths in Matthew 5:21 – 47.

- Jesus introduced each myth with this formula: *You have heard that it was said.*
- Then he busted each myth with this verbal formula: *But I tell you…*

He was contrasting the *myth* to the *truth*. For example, the myth in 5:21 is a religious myth that basically taught this: *God is okay if you hate someone as long as you don't murder them.* Jesus then destroys the myth by saying: *But I say to you, whoever hates his brother has already committed murder.* In God's mind, the only difference between hate and murder is the act. God is *not* okay with hate in our hearts.

My point is this: You can see the Big Idea that emerges from Matthew 5:21 – 47: "Religious Myths Busted by Jesus." Needless to say, it was easy to come up with a series title: "Myth Busters." This is the sermon series, and the four myths yielded four individual sermons:

1. The Myth about Hate
2. The Myth about Bitterness
3. The Myth about Lust
4. The Myth about Divorce

I am writing about this series after it was preached. What I thought would be a lighthearted series turned out to be one of the most sobering I have delivered. Dealing with hate, bitterness, lust, and divorce directly from the Matthew text was powerful and focused, and it changed many lives. I know in my heart that the myths about these subjects were busted for my congregation and that the series will be unforgettable for many.

d. Plan to Create a Series Atmosphere

Creating a series atmosphere elevates the learning experience. This work will be the responsibility of the design team, but the pastor-teacher must embrace the concept. At Christ Fellowship, we seek to strategically design our church campus to reflect each sermon series. A campus that is visually aligned with the sermon series theme will awaken the senses and engage the mind even before teaching is launched.

On a Saturday evening or a Sunday morning, we only have people for about an hour. Their minds need to be in tune with where we are going as soon as possible. If someone walks onto our campus and immediately knows that the message today is about spiritual warfare, I have already engaged their minds and put their thoughts on the right track, and I am ahead of the game. That is simply good stewardship of the time we have.

Outside: Creating a series atmosphere can potentially begin on the outside of the building and move in toward the auditorium. A few cleverly placed objects leading to the auditorium can clue people to the subject matter of what they are about to hear, see, and participate in. Again, start simple. You don't have to be elaborate, but visual objects placed on the path to the worship center can give minds a running start.

A great example of this can be seen at theme parks such as Disney World, Islands of Adventure, and Six Flags. As you stand in line to await certain rides, the creators of the ride create a sense of preparation as you move toward the ride. Props, computer-generated images, and other visual stimulants begin to prepare your mind for the trip even before it begins.

That is what an outside visual does. Some of the people coming to learn God's Word arrive on campus with distracted minds. An argument may have occurred in the car on the way to church. Worries may have taken minds hostage. Pain and discouragement may have someone's mind off kilter. Strategically placed visuals can attract these minds and help put them on the right track before you begin to teach.

Auditorium and stage area: Once inside the auditorium, you can be even more strategic with the stage design. In years past, most stage settings in churches were designed to promote tradition and liturgy. The multisensory revolution is changing that. Its emphasis is *learning*. The stage, therefore, is less concerned with traditions and liturgical icons and more concerned with educational elements. Backgrounds, lighting, screens, and sound take high priority as they elevate the learning experience. The goal, of course, is to communicate God's Word, and the stage is viewed as a communication tool.

Stage design has to do with setting a stage with visual cues that highlight the theme of the text or the topic you will be teaching. Props, graphics, screens, and art become strategic tools for generating interest, creating mental understanding, and making a series unforgettable. A well-designed stage can assist the teacher in grabbing audience attention and help keep the audience's mind focused on the main thing.

The size of your stage and the room will determine how elaborate you can get. At Christ Fellowship, three of our campuses are blessed with relatively large platforms. The other two are smaller. We have learned to be flexible.

Stage design is less of a science and more of an art. It's a lot like interior design. In fact, some of the best stage designers have gifts in interior design, graphic design, and art. This is a ministry for those who have the capacity to dream, visualize, arrange, and place.

There are people with these skills hidden within your church. You may have to draw them out. Retired people, stay-at-home moms, or those simply with a knack for design can be a great asset to this kind of work. They will be honored to come to your aid.

e. Marry the Series Theme to the Worship

Worship and Bible teaching are inseparable theological disciplines. They should never be divorced from one another. Instead, they should be married — like a couple that is meant to be together. When worship and biblical teaching are married as one seamless force, the synergy is powerful and the effect is dramatic. In order to synchronize teaching and worship, the worship pastor should work closely with the design team.

Under his or her leadership, voices, instruments, lighting, sound, and other elements should be combined to create one seamless experience between worship and teaching. If executed correctly, it will be like a seamless piece of carpet. The congregation will not sense a seam between the two experiences.

At Christ Fellowship, our worship pastors have assembled *worship design teams.* Just as I have a teaching design team, they have a worship design team. These two teams work in harmony and brainstorm to create a worship and teaching experience that is built around the theme of the biblical text.

f. Plan to Connect the Series to Small Groups

To reap the full impact of the sermon series, make plans to incorporate the series into all your small groups. At Christ Fellowship, we often produce a daily devotional for our small groups that matches the flow of the sermon series. This creates alignment in our worship and our small groups. The effect is a church-wide sense of unity.

For example, we just finished a series entitled "The Pursuit of Happiness." This series was based on the Beatitudes from Matthew 5. During this series, our small groups were aligned with the flow of the five-part sermon sequence. Daily devotions were developed around each weekly theme. The synergy generated by having the entire church on the same sheet is nothing short of thrilling! I could hear conversations permeating the campuses, and the conversations were about the same subject.

It is also wise to connect the series to all age-graded ministries. When we launch a series in the adult worship areas, the student worship areas follow the same theme. Though they dream up their own creative messages, we are all on the same page. The net effect of this is a "sameness of thought" throughout the campus. The end product is powerful and creates a deep sense of oneness throughout our church.

g. Plan to Promote the Series

As a teacher, you put a lot of hard work into your messages. In order to get the greatest mileage out of your work, it makes sense to promote the series. Get the word out that you are going to tackle an issue that people need to learn about. Just as visual teaching raises attention levels, so does visual promotion. There are many creative ways to visually promote a series. Here are a few ideas:

- sermon logos
- business cards with sermon logo as an invitation to attend
- mail-outs with sermon logo and an invitation to attend
- wristbands with sermon logo
- key chain attachments with a Scripture verse from the series

In addition, link the end of one series to the upcoming series. In other words, as you end one series, begin to promote the next series. It's like chain-smoking. When I was a kid, my dad would smoke a cigarette all the way to the filter. Just before he finished, however, he would light a new one with the one he was finishing.

That's the idea here. As you draw one series to a close, begin to light the fire on the next one. If you have a great Easter series, don't let attendance drop after Easter. Plan to keep the growth going by promoting the next series. This year we are doing an Easter series called "Master-Peace." On Easter Sunday, we will have a huge promotion for the upcoming series called "The Dirty Dozen."

h. Establish Series Objectives

Teaching God's Word is a mission, and any mission must have clearly established objectives. Establishing those objectives is the work and responsibility of the teacher. In other words, the teacher must determine the desired outcomes of the series. As you unpack the series, where do you plan to take the audience, and what do you want them to do when they get there? Remember, our goal is to produce "doers of the Word," not hearers only. Therefore, we have to determine ahead of time what we want them to do.

For example, in the series "Unwrapping Christmas," we had several outcomes in mind, and our teaching team came to the design team with these desired objectives. Realizing that many lost people would be present at our Christmas services, we wanted to accomplish the following four objectives:

1. Demonstrate to lost people that the Christian faith is not blind faith, but that it is faith based on evidence and proof. I wanted unsaved people to come away with the sense that Christianity is built on a solid foundation of substance and evidence. I wanted to convince them that the Christian faith is proven by the facts

of science, physiology, archaeology, history, and verbal predictive prophecy.

2. Demonstrate to Christians the same facts in order to bolster their confidence and faith in the Word of God and in Christ Jesus.
3. Prepare people for the attacks that accuse Christianity of being a blind faith.
4. Become an eyewitness to the salvation of people based on the above strategy.

Our teaching team came to the design team early on with the series theme/title and these series objectives. This gave them a running start on designing a Christmas multisensory experience. It was an amazing Christmas, and our attendance soared to numbers never before seen in our church. The pastors developed the sermon series, but the design team made it sense-sational. Their visual and interactive imaginations helped make it compelling, clear, and unforgettable.

i. Establish Series Parameters

Before you take the series theme to your design team, be sure to determine the parameters of the series. How many messages will be in the series? What will be the topics of the sermons be? For example, in the above-mentioned Christmas series, the design team knew it would be a four-part series. The messages would be an exposition of Matthew 1 – 2 and would deal with the following theological subjects:

1. Evidence from Christ's genealogy
2. Evidence from Christ's virgin birth
3. Evidence from messianic prophecies
4. Evidence from a relationship with God

Such information makes the process objective. It demonstrates to your teams that you know where you are going in the series. The design team now knows the series theme, the number of messages, and the topics to be covered in the series. Providing such information demonstrates leadership. Your team will appreciate it.

j. Plan to Evaluate Series Results

At the conclusion of each message and each series, the pastors, teaching team, and design team should meet to discuss the outcomes. Questions asked about the above series were:

1. Was the evidence persuasive?
2. Did unsaved people embrace Christ?
3. Did the evidence encourage God's people?
4. Are God's people better prepared for attacks on the faith?

Making such honest evaluations allows us to examine what we did right and what we need to correct or improve on. We always allow for open discussion and suggestions as long as it is done in a spirit of love and encouragement.

STEP 2: DETERMINE INDIVIDUAL SERMONS

Once the theme of a sermon series is determined, it is time to determine the individual sermons. There are several essential elements in this part of the process.

a. Let the Sermon Flow from Scripture

Just as the sermon series must emerge from the Scriptures, so too must the individual sermons. Follow the structure of God's Word and allow God to speak to you and to the congregation through the logical flow of the text. Needless to say, the teacher will have to demonstrate intellectual knowledge at this point. Don't let that scare you off. Your people can handle an intellectually stimulating sermon.

Bible expositors tend to be efficient at this part of the work. Their seminary training in the biblical languages and hermeneutics makes them efficient at communicating the content of the text. At the same time, however, they tend to be weak on the communication side of the equation.

b. Look for the Big Idea of the Sermon

Just as you must identify the Big Idea of the sermon series, you must also identify the Big Idea of the individual sermon. The Big Idea is the main thought you want people to take away from the sermon. For example, we are planning a series from Matthew 8 – 9 that will be entitled "Master-Peace." In the gospel of Matthew, Jesus offers to establish the kingdom. The kingdom will be a time on earth when four kinds of peace will be established:

1. Peace in nature
2. Peace in the spirit-demon dimension
3. Peace in disease
4. Peace in death

To demonstrate that Jesus is the Prince of Peace, he visually demonstrates his power to bring:

1. Peace over nature (calming the storm)
2. Peace over demons (casting out the demons)
3. Peace over disease (healing the woman)
4. Peace over death (raising the dead child)

Thus, the Big Idea of the series is "Master-Peace," and four Big Idea sermon titles have emerged:

1. Christ Brings Peace in and over Natural Disaster
2. Christ Brings Peace in and over Spiritual Warfare
3. Christ Brings Peace in and over Disease
4. Christ Brings Peace in and over Death

c. Plan to Make the Sermon Multisensory

Not only can your design team assist you in making the series multisensory, but they can also help make the individual sermons multisensory. Keep in mind, the sooner you can provide them with information pertaining to the sermon topics, the sooner they can begin to brainstorm ways to make it multisensory.

For example, the teaching team at Christ Fellowship worked on a series entitled "iPray," an exposition of the Lord's Prayer in Matthew 6. It focused on the simplicity of prayer. We gave our design team the six topics for development:

1. Our Father: *Prayer is Relational*
2. Thy Kingdom Come: *Prayer Puts This Life in Eternal Perspective*
3. Give Us: *Our Father Provides Our Daily Needs*
4. Forgive Us: *Our Father Is Characterized by Mercy and Forgiveness*
5. Lead Us: *Our Father Leads Us and Delivers Us*
6. For Yours Is the Kingdom: *Our Father Is in Control*

Ideas began churning for the verbal, visual, and interactive presentation of this series. Props and visuals included fathers, children, fetus ultra sounds, the cancellation of debt, navigation, and many others.

STEP 3: BRAINSTORM FOR MULTISENSORY COMMUNICATION

Once the teacher or teachers have determined the series theme and sermon topics, it is time for the design team to go to work. Their assignment is to brainstorm ways to transform the series and sermons into a unique multisensory learning experience. Creating a stage setting, visual aids, props, campus atmosphere, lighting, screen designs, and extraordinary worship sets are all on the "to do" list of the design team. It is now time for effective brainstorming.

Effective brainstorming is the act of throwing all sorts of ideas on the table for consideration and coming up with the best idea. Obviously, the more creative minds you involve in the process, the more effective the process will be.

Be warned: Many brainstorming sessions turn out to be rain-storming sessions that result in mental washouts. There is little direction, and the result is hours of random ideas that lead to mental fatigue and creative frustration. Brainstorming can be effective and fun if you have the right ingredients. The following is a list of the essential ingredients for effective barnstorming:

a. Schedule a Brainstorming Time

If you have a team to help you brainstorm ideas, you will need a specific time to conduct your sessions. If you don't schedule your brainstorming sessions, they won't happen. Only what is scheduled gets done.

This raises the question about timing for brainstorming. I have found evening brainstorming to be ineffective. The reason is simple; people are tired and their creative juices are drained. Mornings or early afternoons are the optimum time. Our minds are rested, our creativity is at the highest, and production is at a maximum. For this reason, your team will need to be comprised of people who can gather at those times. This is why stay-at-home mothers, retired individuals, and people with flexible schedules are your best choices.

b. Provide a Brainstorming Room

Not only must we have a time that promotes creativity, but also a place. In other words, the room itself must foster a mindset of imagination. A room that is bland or has the feel of a boardroom will squelch ingenuity and creativity. But a room that puts people face to face with other creative minds and creative tools is a greenhouse for wonderful ideas.

I suggest a room that has round tables, lots of pens and crayons, and a whiteboard to collect ideas for consideration. Such a room sends a message to the team that this is a place to release your imagination. We often use our children's area for these meetings.

c. Locate Creative Minds

Creative teams without creative minds will only create problems. If you put together a creative team, you must choose your team members wisely.

Look for people who have the capacity to dream. Artistic people, graphic designers, engineers, interior designers, and marketing strategists tend to be creative in their own right. Find them, recruit them, and use them for the glory of God.

Also, be sure to recruit people who are not overly sensitive to criticism. Some ideas will get rejected, and an overly sensitive person may find it difficult to cope with criticism and rejection. Choose your design team wisely. Invest in their training. Taking them to a conference on multisensory communication can pay huge dividends in the long run.

d. Ensure Creative Freedom

If you are brainstorming as a team, the leader of the design team must make sure there is an atmosphere of expressive freedom — a climate that fosters creative thinking and creative release. There also must be a pervasive attitude that says, "We can make it happen." All it takes is one "killjoy" in the room to stifle other people's creative ideas. In other words, if people's ideas repeatedly get shot down, they will inexorably shut down.

Yes, it is healthy to challenge one another's ideas, but it must be done in a way that is not judgmental and discouraging. Such challenges, if done in the right spirit, are healthy to the process. Keep this protocol in mind: Agree to withhold challenge until all ideas are in. After all the ideas are submitted, find a positive way to evaluate them and select the best. One way to accomplish this is to list all ideas on a whiteboard and then vote on the best.

e. Have a Brainstorming Process

You will need to give structure to your brainstorming sessions. Otherwise, they will run off madly in all directions, tire everyone out, and accomplish little. The following structure may be helpful in moving your brainstorming session to useful action steps that can be plugged into the sermon series:

1. Gather around tables with plenty of paper and writing tools.
2. Identify the theme of the series as well as the topics in individual sermons.
3. Let everyone write down his or her ideas for verbal, visual, and interactive illustrations.
4. Give each person one minute to describe their ideas as the leader copies the ideas on a whiteboard.
5. Have the team vote on the best ideas.

6. Pull the best ideas together and put them into action steps for implementation.

f. Focus on Grabbing Audience Attention

Be proactive when it comes to gaining audience attention. The audience cannot act on what they have not paid attention to. If we want people to be "doers of the Word," you have to grab their attention. Moreover, remember that the more senses you stimulate in the teaching, the higher the levels of attention.

With these facts in the forefront, the design team should be strategic in attracting audience attention. Remember the effects of visual stimulation as it relates to gaining attention. The research conclusively demonstrates that attention levels rise when we add visual communication to verbal communication.

Since people tend to get bored quickly, we must hook their attention as quickly as possible. Get visual quickly. In fact, if possible, begin visually. Design a visual illustration that connects to the Big Idea of the sermon and begin your sermon with the visual. This will awaken the senses quickly, and it will help you grab audience attention at the beginning. I can always see people's attention levels heighten when I begin visually.

g. Focus on Establishing Clarity

Clarity is the mother of comprehension, and comprehension is a must for action. People cannot act on what they do not understand. We have two options when it comes to teaching the Bible: Dumb down the message content so that it is understandable, or teach the complex things of the Word, though in a form that ensures clarity.

In-depth theology need not be divorced from contemporary preaching. We do not have to sacrifice intellectualism on the altar of being understood. Theology that is complex and difficult to grasp can be made clear by adding visuals and interactive elements to the teaching. Remember the effects of visual stimulation as it relates to comprehension. The research conclusively demonstrates that comprehension levels rise when we add visual communication to verbal communication.

h. Focus on Making It Unforgettable

Sermons that have that unforgettable touch change lives for a lifetime. As the design team focuses on the teaching, factor in the unforgettable dynamic. Look for creative ways to make the sermon last. Think duct tape — make it stick! Don't forget the effects of visual and interactive stimulation as it relates to mental retention. The research conclusively demonstrates that retention levels rise when we add visual communication to verbal communication.

STEP 4: PLOT ACTION STEPS

Once your design ideas have surfaced and have been fleshed out into objective action steps, it is time to assign tasks to individuals in the room. I suggest you bullet point action steps on an overhead, whiteboard, and the like. Determine the following and write them down:

1. Who is responsible for what?
2. What is the time frame for completion?
3. Who needs to know? Who will let them know?

The following chart shows the flow for implementing multisensory sermons.

STEP 5: ENSURE QUALITY

No one deserves excellence any more than God does. Nothing is more repulsive than having to sit through a service that is rife with mistakes in planning, mistakes in execution, and outright poor quality. In order to ensure quality, the three following suggestions may help:

a. Make Sure the Worship REEKS

At Christ Fellowship we use the acronym REEKS[1] to ensure the quality of everything we do in terms of teaching and worship. Before we launch a series and a sermon, we filter it through this grid and ask the appropriate questions.

Relevant: The first question we ask ourselves has to do with relevance. The Scriptures are always relevant, but teachers can have an uncanny knack for making them seem irrelevant. As teachers we must take what happened two thousand years ago and bring it into our current situation. We have to ask ourselves before we go forth: Does this connect to people's lives?

Excellence: If anyone deserves excellence, it is God. If anyone deserves our best, it is God. Consequently, we always ask ourselves the question of excellence. Will the teaching presentation bear the marks of solid preparation and delivery? Will people walk away thinking to themselves, "Wow, those people give God the best"?

CHRIST FELLOWSHIP FLOW CHART FOR IMPLEMENTING MULTISENSORY SERIES AND MULTISENSORY SERMONS

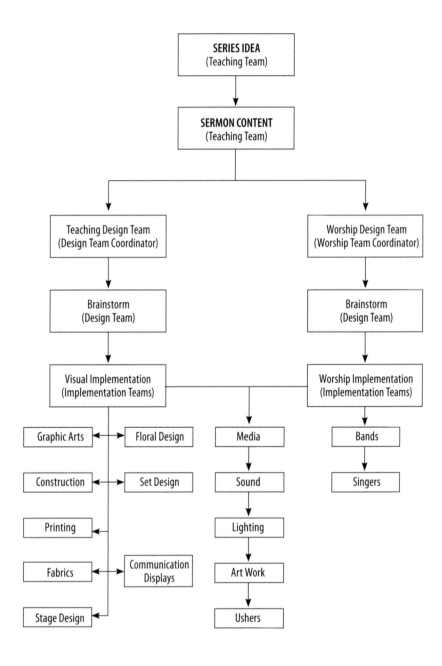

MULTISENSORY IMPLEMENTATION STEPS

Series Theme_____Date: _____to _____

This Week's Sermon Title _____

CONSTRUCTION ACTIONS

1. List items that will need to be constructed or purchased to complete stage design, campus props, and sermon illustrations:

    a. _____   c. _____   e. _____

    b. _____   d. _____   f. _____

2. Who will be responsible, and what are they responsible for? _____

    _____

3. What is the time frame for completion? _____

TECHNICAL ACTIONS

1. Check which technical resources will be involved?

    ☐ Special Lighting   ☐ Special Videos

    ☐ Others   ☐ Special Sound

2. How will they be involved? _____

VISUAL ARTS AND GRAPHIC ACTIONS

1. Check which technical resources will be involved?

    ☐ Screen graphics

    ☐ Paintings or Sculpting

2. Who will make it happen? _____

PEOPLE ACTIONS

1. Check which people resources will be involved? How so?

    ☐ Band   ☐ Singers   ☐ Drama Team

    ☐ Stage helpers   ☐ Greeters   ☐ Traffic

    ☐ Welcome Center Team   ☐ Guest Reception Team

Engaging: The third question has to do with the boredom factor. Will this series and this sermon engage the minds for the audience? Will it quickly hook the congregation's attention and hold it for the duration of the teaching?

Kreative: This question has to do with variety and the factor of being unpredictable. In terms of the music and the teaching style, is there a sense of uniqueness?

Seamless: This final question deals with the issue of flow. Nothing hinders worship any more than starting and stopping. Engaging people in worship is like trying to get an airplane airborne. We are trying to lift people out of the horizontal dimension and into the vertical dimension. When the worship has a seamless feel to it, it is like an airplane achieving liftoff.

b. Take the Time to Rehearse

If you are depending on other people to help execute the worship service, it is always wise to gather before the service and go over the procedures. Just as our musicians rehearse before they perform in order to ensure a seamless presentation, it is wise for the teacher to rehearse with the team before the message presentation. This does not have to last long; just quickly run over the process.

This is an "all hands on deck" kind of rehearsal. Anyone involved in that week's sermon production should be present: worship leader, lighting, cameras, video, sound, prop coordinators, drama team, and so on. At Christ Fellowship we meet two hours prior to our Saturday evening service (i.e., at 4:30 p.m.). This one-time rehearsal will suffice for all the following services. A quick rehearsal can cover a multitude of sins.

c. Take the Time to Evaluate Quality

One of the most difficult actions we take as a staff at Christ Fellowship is the post-evaluation of all of our services. Before we discuss the upcoming sermon and worship service, we first evaluate the past week's service. We look at the worship and the teaching through the REEKS grid.

Sometimes such honest evaluations can be painful, but the positives far outweigh the negatives. By looking at what we did right and what we did wrong, we are able to reinforce what we did right and correct what we did wrong. It always has a way of making us better than before.

DISCUSSION QUESTIONS

1. Discuss how topics can be generated from a book of the Bible.

2. Develop a sermon series idea from a selected text.

3. Discuss the entire design process. How will you piece this together?

CHAPTER 9

PROCEDURES:
EFFECTIVE USE OF MULTISENSORY COMPONENTS

Without one's senses, the brain would be like an eternal prisoner locked within the confines of one's skull.

LYNN HAMILTON

Try to determine the context of the following scene: An endless sea of people surrounds a center stage, and on this center stage is the dominant individual of the gathering. Everyone is there to see him and him alone. The stage itself is dominated by a green circular logo, which sets the mood of the gathering.

As you fix your gaze at the stage, bright rays of light flood from its center. In fact, there is an extravaganza of colored light beams. The light has been engineered to radiate through a haze of smoke and then reflect off multifaceted colored stones. What is more, the entire stage floor is strategically designed with crystal glass, which reflects the light to even greater intensity. The effect is an explosion of psychedelic color that is almost blinding to the eyes.

Keep your eyes on the sight, because dominating the scene are scores of musicians, all playing musical instruments. The music and singing are so loud that a reporter on the scene (John Patmos) describes the noise levels as *"megale phone"* (megaphone-like). The throng of people gathering around the one on the center stage is ecstatic with excitement and anticipation.

Now, where are you? What is the context? Are you at a rock concert? Are you at a very contemporary church? Nope! You're actually in heaven! The fact is, I just described the worship in heaven as presented in Revelation 4 and 5. To say the worship in heaven is multisensory is an understatement!

HEAVEN GOES MULTISENSORY

In Revelation 4 and 5, the Word of God takes us into the throne room of God for a view of worship that is done right. This is the actual scene of worship as it happens around the throne of God in heaven, and the dominant characteristics of the worship are *teaching* and *worship.*

God is teaching, and all of heaven responds with worship and praise. Just a casual look at the teaching and you see that one objective dominates the gathering. That objective is to exalt the Son of God and to set in motion the events that will lead up to his inauguration as King of kings and Lord of lords. To communicate that theme to all the inhabitants of heaven, God unleashes a multisensory extravaganza.

The teaching is presented in forms that are verbal, visual, and interactive. To say there is a *wow factor* in heaven's worship is stating it mildly. God aims for multisensory teaching and *big* worship! For those who are accustomed to worship services that are small and bland, heaven will be a huge shock. Look at the scene closely, and you will see the components that set the stage:

- vivid light
- extravagant color
- powerful sound
- new music
- visual communication
- interactive participation

This text gives us a model for the use of multisensory teaching. God selects the theme, which is the glory of the Lamb. God then uses light, color, explicit visuals, new music, and interactive participation to make the teaching compelling, clear, and absolutely unforgettable. Simply stated, God uses a multisensory methodology to teach us about the glory of his Son.

Let's look at the multisensory elements in Revelation 4 and reflect on how to use those same elements to make your teaching compelling, clear, and unforgettable.

Use Lighting to Elevate Worship and Teaching — God Does

To say that "light is a dominant factor in heaven" is an understatement. God is light, God radiates light, God loves light, and God uses light for worship and teaching. In the scene of Revelation 4, the apostle John describes the appearance of God, and it is one of blazing light reflecting and refracting off polished jewels and then off a sea of glass.

- Revelation 4:3: "And the one who sat there had the appearance of *jasper.*" Jasper is a sparkling crystal stone. It is an opaque quartz with multiple colors. Jasper is best known for its capacity to reflect and refract light into a spectrum of beautiful colors.
- Revelation 4:3: "And the one who sat there had the appearance of … *carnelian.*" Carnelian is a dazzling gem with a deep fiery red color. When light shines through carnelian, it has the appearance of being on fire. Get the picture? John is describing the light of God, and it is one of blazing light reflecting and refracting off polished jewels, creating a psychedelic flash of color.
- Revelation 4:6: "And before the throne there was what looked like a sea of glass, clear as crystal." God cranks up the light even more. Beneath his throne, on the stage floor as it were, is a sea of glass. That massive sea of glass is there for one purpose — to reflect the color and light into greater intensity.

Incidentally, the view of God's throne from Isaiah 6 shows smoke rising like a haze from God's presence. It is a supernatural laser light show! John MacArthur writes in his book on heaven, "All this emphasis on brightness and clarity suggests that heaven is not a land of shadows and mists."[1]

This looks like a modern day rock concert! Bright lights, multicolored lights, haze, loud music, and loud singing. If this seems over the top, it is not. No one is more occupied with light and color than God himself. God is a spirit, but when God puts on his clothes so to speak, he puts on light — and not just any light: blinding, piercing, penetrating, colorful light!

Today, many churches create worship and teaching services that radiate light — and lots of it. At Christ Fellowship, we use all sorts of colored lights that are reflected through haze to intensify the color, the brightness, and the effect. Our goal is to mirror the light of Revelation 4 as close as possible. We cannot achieve that level of light, but we can honor God by trying.

Needless to say, many churches that use such lighting have been criticized for mimicking a rock concert. But when a church service is filled with light, color, and powerful music, it is not mimicking the world; it is imitating the worship of God as it occurs in heaven. It's a sad reality, but often the world does a better job at creating an environment of worship than the church does. The world gives *big worship* to their little gods, while the church often gives *small worship* to our big God. Come on, church! We should not let the world hijack the kind of worship and teaching that God designed for Christian worship. Let's take it back for God!

By the way, it seems as if our ancestors did the best they could to generate light in worship. They did not have electric power, but they did have candles, and they lit as many as possible. Later, they figured out how to create glass that could reflect that light into multiple colors — they called it stained glass. Today, God has given us so much more light capacity, and I believe our ancestors would encourage us to use it as powerfully as possible.

Lighting is not only a factor in worship; it is also a factor in teaching. Anyone who works in the realm of education understands the importance of proper lighting. During the teaching at Christ Fellowship, we use colored lights to create a variety of background effects on the stage. The colors are preselected and intended to reflect the theme of the message. At the same time, the lights in the audience are brought up as bright as possible. Since we are committed to teaching the Scriptures, we want our people to be able to read the Bible and to fill in their listening guide during the teaching. An auditorium that is left dim during the teaching makes reading the Bible and taking notes difficult for the congregation.

The sum of this is this: Good lighting must be used strategically, not randomly. Gone are the days of just flipping the light switch. Lighting should be used tactfully to create a meditation environment when we are worshiping, and it must be used strategically to create a learning environment when we are teaching.

At Christ Fellowship, this translates into a whole ministry of individuals who manage our lighting. Our lighting is divided into two parts: *worship lighting* and *teaching lighting*. Worship lighting at Christ Fellowship is multifaceted and seeks to create the *wow* factor of Revelation 4. To capture that kind of glorious color in our worship, we have made a considerable investment in our worship lighting. Our teaching lighting has one primary goal: Illuminate the stage and auditorium in order to elevate the teaching effect.

Use Sound to Elevate Your Teaching

To say that the worship in heaven is loud and powerful is also no exaggeration. The voice and thunder of God rumbles throughout the teaching, and the people respond with loud singing. In heaven, it is obvious that God puts a premium on quality sound, and the reason is simple: Phenomenal teaching requires great sound!

I am convinced that some teachers are only "good teachers" because they teach in an environment that has poor sound. To elevate your teaching level, attention must be given to sound. We must focus not only on the sense of seeing and interaction, but even more so on the sense of hearing. Remember, ours is a spoken message. Visuals, interaction, and other sensory teaching elements are only *support* for the spoken word. Let us never forget that we are teachers first, and we must be heard clearly.

Gone are the days of ornate buildings with cheap sound systems. The multisensory revolution has elevated teaching to its proper place in the church. As a result, elaborate sound takes priority over elaborate buildings. Our mission is to build lives, not buildings, and we need sound to do that.

Great sound not only elevates the communication factor; it can also make certain illustrations have more impact. When we are showing videos, we always make sure the sound is appropriate for the effect we wish to generate. The sound is adjusted to accommodate the teaching point.

For example, I was once teaching on the blazing glory of God as it appears in the book of Revelation. To illustrate that glory, I showed a nighttime launch of the space shuttle in high definition visual and high definition sound. The effect was amazing. The light generated in the auditorium by the shuttle liftoff was incredibly bright. But if the visual effect was powerful, the sound effect was off the chart! We elevated the sound to capture the power of the shuttle as it came to life on the launching pad. As the engines of the shuttle ignited, the room began to quake, and when the solid rockets exploded with power, the auditorium felt like it was going to fall in on itself. It was so thunderous, that a light fixture actually fell from the ceiling. People thought we planned it that way for effect. We didn't, but did people get some idea of the power and light and glory of God!

Use Fresh Music to Stimulate the Sixth Sense

One glimpse of the worship in heaven and you immediately get the idea that God likes light in worship. That same scene of worship also demonstrates that God likes "new songs." Revelation 5:9 says, "And they sang a new song." Why? Because when biblical teaching and new music are married together, they complement one another.

This is the very theme that has given rise to modern Christian music. For centuries people sang the same songs over and over again. There is nothing wrong with them. They touched people's lives. But they were often sung without passion because they were not fresh in their minds. They were expected. Interestingly, many of these old songs are now being dusted off, freshened up with a new sound, and sung to touch the hearts of a new generation.

The point is this: When fresh music is married to the Word of God, the impact has a way of touching our souls. Nothing prepares the soul for biblical teaching like music that is new and fresh.

When our musicians and singers bring forth music that is fresh, unexpected, and powerful, it prepares the hearts of people for teaching as few forces can.

THE POWER OF MULTISENSORY ILLUSTRATIONS

Early in chapter 1 of this book this diagram was designed to grab your attention. Remember this image?

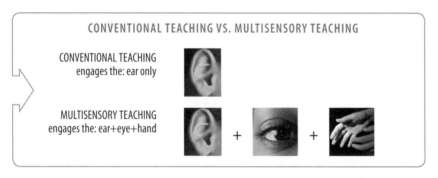

This is the goal of going visual when you are teaching God's Word. The purpose is to arouse the senses, which are the conduit to the brain, and then to engage the mind into the subject matter being presented. Visuals help garner attention, clarify the teaching, and foster long-term memory.

This, however, raises the question of execution. How can we transform a lecture-only sermon into a sermon that contains visuals? The number of ways is limitless. The only limit is your ability to imagine. Here are a few simple guidelines:

Transform Verbal Illustrations into Visual Illustrations

Here's a great rule of thumb for coming up with multisensory illustrations: If you can talk about it, you can probably make it visual. Many of my favorite multisensory illustrations simply meant turning verbal illustrations into visual and interactive illustrations. The best way to describe this process is simply to provide you with an example of what I am talking about.

Reaching children for Christ has been an all-consuming passion for me. Two years ago, I gave two messages to Christ Fellowship about a strategy to make that happen in Miami. My goal was to create a "Disney-like atmosphere" for our children at Christ Fellowship. I envisioned a place that would be so exciting that children would *beg* parents to bring them to church. I wanted to take the wonderful truths of Christ and put them on a level that a child could embrace and love. Much of what is taught in our adult services is not on the level of a child. Our goal was to create a children's space in which the love of Jesus would be brought down to their level.

To communicate this vision to the adults, who would need to fork out a lot of money, I taught about Jesus and the children — specifically the passage where Jesus knelt down to pick up a child. What an image — Jesus stooping to the level of a little boy or little girl.

To give a visual of this, I had a real basketball hoop complete with backboard placed on the stage. The basketball rim was placed at the adult level — ten feet high. We then brought several three- and four-year-olds onto the stage. I was going to teach them *how* to play basketball. I gave a demonstration in which I tossed the ball into the basket for a goal. I then asked each child to follow my example. Needless to say, not one of them could throw the ball that high. Then, we brought a basketball expert onto the stage and asked him to teach the children how to do it. Even after an expert showed them how to throw the ball into the ten-foot basket, not one of them was able to do so. The problem was not with the teachers; the problem was that the hoop was too high.

We then *visually* demonstrated a novel idea. The hoop apparatus was adjustable, and we simply lowered it to a child's level. Now, with the hoop at a child's level, each child was able to participate and to learn about basketball. Little boys and little girls were laughing and playing basketball on our stage. When the goal was too high, it was frustrating for the children. Once it was lowered to their level, it was not only reachable, it was fun!

In the past I would have only told that illustration. I would have tried to communicate with words only. But it was easy to transform that verbal illustration into a visual illustration. This was an interactive illustration as the children participated with me. Which do you think was better at capturing attention? Which made the point clearer? Which was more memorable?

The Max Factor

One of my favorite writers is Max Lucado. Max can paint a picture with words that is so moving and so powerful that they often move me to tears or laughter. I have found, however, that I can transform some of Max's verbal illustrations into multisensory illustrations. This is possible with all good writers. Here is an example.

In a series on calling, I wanted to demonstrate that God has given each of us different skills and abilities that enable us to serve him. I wanted to make it clear that we must focus on what God has given to us and not on what he has given to others. This particular message was from our study in Matthew, part of a series entitled: "24: Your Daily Calling."

As I approached this message, I recalled reading a story from one of Max's books entitled *Cure for the Common Life*. Let me quote a portion of the story, and then I will tell you how I transformed it into a visual illustration.

> Tucked away in the cedar chest of my memory is the image of a robust and rather rotund children's Bible teacher in a small West Texas church. Here's why I tell you about her. She enjoyed giving each of us a can of crayons and a sketch of Jesus torn from a coloring book. We each had our own can, mind you, reassigned from cupboard duty to classroom. What had held peaches or spinach now held a dozen or so Crayolas. "Take the crayons I gave you," she would instruct us, "and color Jesus." And so we would.
>
> We didn't illustrate pictures of ourselves; we colored the Son of God. We didn't pirate crayons from other cans, we used what she gave us. This was the fun of it. "Do the best you can with what you get." No blue for the sky? Make it purple. If Jesus hair is blonde instead of brown, the teacher won't mind. She loaded the can. She taught us to paint Jesus with our own colors.
>
> God made you to do likewise. He loaded your can. He made you unique. The next few chapters have one message: color Christ with the crayons God gave you.[2]

What a word picture! To transform Max's *word* picture into a live *visual* was simple. The following is a written manuscript of the sermon I gave based on that verbal image. It began with a group of little children joining me on stage as the message began. By the way, the children on stage immediately grabbed everyone's attention.

These are some little children from our children's ministry. Jesus often used little children to teach "grownups" profound truths, didn't he? And that's exactly what I hope to do today. I want to use these children to teach us "grownups" a compelling truth about our calling from God. The illustration I am about to demonstrate comes from Max Lucado's book *Cure for the Common Life*, but man is it a powerful picture.

> Now, let me tell you how we set this up. Last weekend during their small group, each of these children was given a coloring book outline of Jesus. Their assignment from the teacher was to color that picture of Jesus. They were to take their picture of Jesus and color it as beautifully as they could.
>
> And get this: To enable them to fulfill that "calling," their teacher gave each child his or her own can of Crayolas. O yeah: Cans that once held peaches, now held crayons. Cans that once contained beans, were now loaded with varying shades of colors. By the way, some of the crayons weren't perfect. Some had a nub end, some were broken, and that was okay.
>
> But this was key to the assignment: Each child's can of Crayolas was different from their other classmates' cans. Nobody's was the same. Mind you, everybody had a can of crayons, but everybody had a different arrangement of colors that was uniquely theirs. And the assignment was this: "Take the crayons that have been given to you and color Jesus." And so they did: Take a look: [The children show their pictures of Jesus.] [Applause.]
>
> Now, let me turn a corner and draw an analogy to that, because God created you to do the same thing. God created you to color the glory to Christ with your life. To enable you to pull off this assignment, he loaded your life with a colorful arrangement of skills, talents, and spiritual gifts that are uniquely yours.

Was that example ever powerful! Incidentally, at the conclusion of the message, we gave another powerful visual about using what you have been given to glorify Christ. A young lady in our church who has been a quadriplegic from birth gave a visual testimony about how God was able to use her in spite of her broken body to bring glory to him. Like a broken crayon can be used to color Christ, so can a broken body. It was so powerful because it was so visual!

How to Find Compelling Illustrations

The pressure to find compelling illustrations each week is just another one of the pressures that make teaching so difficult. If you are like me, it is a never-ending challenge, and yet it is one on which great teaching depends. But how do we come up with fresh illustrations, ones that can be transformed into visual illustrations?

The temptation is to resort to illustration books and canned illustrations. They are easy to find and they are prewritten to connect. We know, however, that such "canned" illustrations lack the power of fresh and personal illustrations that come from everyday life.

One suggestion is to look for things in life that arouse your own emotions. As you go through the normal course of living, mark those things that arouse your emotions — good or bad. Look for things in your life that excite you, that bother you, that make you angry, and so on.

Second, ransack past experiences that may shed light on some great truth of God. Such experiences tend to connect people to you personally and then relationally. Perhaps the best way to describe this process is to provide you with an example of what I am talking about.

This past week, my septic tank backed up and began to dump raw sewage into our house. To say this bothered me is putting it mildly! To have raw sewage in your house is a health hazard, because it pollutes the environment of your home. The plumber gave me the news. He said, "Rick, your entire septic tank and drainage field will have to be dug up and replaced at a cost of about 8K." That bothered me even more! It was amazing, however, how this connected to the message I was scheduled to bring that week.

I was teaching part 3 of a series called "Myth Busters" from Matthew 5. In this text, Jesus warns us about lust and pornography. Lust and porn are not harmless forms of entertainment; they are dangerous forms of pollution that disease our very hearts. Jesus says: "Anyone who looks at a woman lustfully has already committed adultery with her in his *heart*" (Matthew 5:28). The emphasis is on our heart and its health. In other words, the danger of lust is that it pollutes you at the very core of your person — your heart.

Jesus' solution to lust is to deal with it drastically. His advice is in the next verse (v. 29): "If your right eye causes you to sin, gouge it out." Now, is Jesus advocating bodily mutilation? Is he literally telling us to gouge out our eyes to prevent us from lusting? No, but he is saying this: "Deal drastically with lust. Get it out of your heart and take drastic measures to do so."

To illustrate this point, I filmed my septic tank as it was being dug up, and I spoke to my congregation standing by the septic tank. The video was projected on the screens, and this is what I said to Christ Fellowship.

> Hello everybody, I am standing here in my front yard. You're probably wondering what's up with the huge hole in the ground? Well, this is my septic tank … oh yeah! I have raw sewage backing up in my house. I tried everything I could to fix the problem myself, but no luck. I tried Drano, a plumbers snake, etc., but with no success. Finally, I called the plumber. He told me they were going to have to dig up my yard, pull out my tank, and replace it along with the entire drainage field. Then, to make matters worse, the cost would be 8K.
>
> In desperation, I asked him, "Is there an easier way to do this? Is there something less drastic than digging up the entire septic tank?" This was his answer: "Mr. Blackwood, if you want that sewage out of your house, it will take drastic measures." Folks, that is precisely what Jesus is saying in this text. If you want the sewage out of your heart, you are going to have to deal with lust drastically.

Mind you: I could have merely told the congregation about my septic tank. Standing by it, however, and letting them see it visually made it compelling, clarifying, and unforgettable.

"Picture It" with Screens

Screens are the new sensation for teaching the Word, and they are becoming more and more affordable. How you place them and how you use them depends on your strategy for communication. At Christ Fellowship we use two side screens and one main center screen. This allows us to split the screens into two uses.

During the teaching, the center screen, which is our large dominant screen, is used to reflect the series logo. The logo is reflected on the screen directly behind the speaker, and this keeps the current message in context of the overall series. This models the teaching of God in Revelation 4. A full circular rainbow dominates heaven's center stage. God gave the half circular rainbow to remind us of his mercy. This full circle rainbow in heaven will be a constant reminder of God's mercy and forgiveness for those who belong to his Son.

In the same spirit, many churches use a center scene logo to communicate the major theme of the teaching. For example, in the series on war, the center screen projected the War logo throughout the entire teaching series. When Eric or I taught on "greed," the big logo on the screen behind us kept "greed" in the context of the series theme, which was "spiritual warfare." The side screens are used to project the image of the speaker as well as Scripture texts and notes.

Screens also give the added dimension of being able to use videos. Frequently, I am able to take our congregation on a field trip of sorts by way of video. I have filmed parts of my sermons at rivers, oceans, my home, courtrooms, in a car while driving, in the forest, by a campfire, on a roller coaster, and so on. As indicated earlier in this chapter, I have shown space shuttle launches complete with powerful light and sound. Such variety and sensory components keep a sermon alive with excitement and unpredictability. Besides, it's fun!

During the musical part of the worship, the center screen is used to create an environment of contemplation. Various software applications display scenes that are reflective and generate a sense of worship. The side screens, of course, display the lyrics to the music.

Some churches opt for one huge central screen. Granger Church in South Bend, Indiana, is a classic example of the power of one dominate screen. They use it effectively for worship and teaching. I recommend a look at their website for an idea of its impact.

Using Art to Elevate Teaching and Worship

I never dreamed of the impact art can have on a worship service. One of the most powerful and mind-blowing worship experiences I have been a part of was when we invited artists to paint during the worship services (see the full account in chapter 7).

Object Lessons: "Show and Tell Time"

Using object lessons is one of the easiest and most effective methods of going visual and interactive. The key to object lesson use is to make it seem natural and seamless to the message. For example, in a series on worry, I walked onto the stage with a laptop in my hand. I compared our minds to a laptop computer and then projected a graphic war game on the screens. The war game was illustrative of the wars that rage inside our heads.

In another message in the same series, I walked onto the stage with a golf club in my hand. I simply spoke about how tension in your arms and wrist will rob a golf swing of its power. The key to generating power in a golf swing is to relax the muscles so you can make a full turn in your wind up and then release the energy stored up in the coil. I was able to give a visual of that with the golf club in my hand. What a picture of how much stress can affect us in life! Mental stress robs us of the power to live a life that is filled with joy. Again, simple objects can grab attention, clarify truth, and make your teaching unforgettable at little cost to you in terms of time and energy.

Using Video Clips to Elevate Teaching

Using videos has been one of the most effective ways to gain attention, make a point clearer, and to create long-term memory. Let me provide two examples.

Field of Dreams. In a sermon on prayer and intimacy with God (the "iPray" series), I wanted to express the notion that God simply wants to be "with us." He simply wants to talk to us, just as a loving father would. To set this up, I walked onto the stage with two baseball gloves in my hand and told the following story from my childhood.

> One of my fondest childhood memories was playing catch with my father. Get the picture: Dad would come home from work, and I'd be lying across the bed in our tiny apartment, reading a comic book or something. But my dad would knock at the door of my room—the door was never closed, but he would knock on the threshold to get my attention.
>
> I can picture it to this day, because he would always have two baseball gloves in hand—one for me, and one for him. And he would always give me this invitation. "Want to catch?" I would jump to my feet and grab my glove, and my father and I would stand outside and throw the ball back and forth till the sun went down.
>
> Mind you: For my dad, he didn't just want to throw the ball. Throwing the ball was simply a point of connection with his child. I would chatter away to my father. I would talk about school, baseball, friends, and anything that came to my mind. Don't miss this: My father didn't necessarily care what I talked about. I am sure it all sounded very immature and childish. He didn't care. He just wanted to be with me and hear me talk to him.
>
> What a picture of God and us! God says to us [Rev. 3:20]: "Here I am! I stand at the door and knock." Now when someone knocks at the door of our house we may ask ourselves, "What does that person want from me?" And we may ask the same question of God. God knocks at the door of our heart, and we may ask God, "God, what do you want from me?" God tells us clearly: "Here I am! I stand at the door and knock. If anyone hears my voice and opens the door, I will come in and eat with him, and he with me."
>
> You see, it's not what God wants *from* us; it's what God wants *for* us. And what does he want for us? He wants a relationship with us. Andy Stanley says of this verse: "There are no more intimate words that Jesus could have tagged onto the end of that statement."[3] When someone invited you to eat with him or her in biblical days, it was an invitation to fellowship together. In other words, if we open that door of our heart, God simply wants to talk with us. If he were knocking at the door of a little boy, he might say to that child: "Want to catch?"

To make this point even more poignant, I closed with a clip from the movie *Field of Dreams*. The basic story line is this: It's about a father who desired to have a relationship with his son — a relationship that would be built around the game of baseball. The father had actually played semipro ball when he was a young man. But now that he had a son, the father simply wanted to connect to his son by "having a catch." He just wanted to spend time with his son, throwing the ball together and talking together.

But when the son became a teenager, he thought his father was uncool. He thought his father was out of touch, and so he rejected the relationship his father wanted to have with him. He would never join his father in a time of catch, and that broke his father's heart. As time went by, the father died, and the son never got a chance to make that right. Later in his life, that grieved the son to no end. It brought pain to his heart that could never be eased.

But in the movie, the son is given another chance. He is given the opportunity to reconnect with his father by building a baseball field in the middle of a cornfield. The voice said: "If you build it, they will come." (I played that scene on the screen). And when Ray builds this field, all these players from the past show up. Shoeless Joe Jackson, Mel Lott, and others come back from the dead to play ball. (This is not a movie to formulate theology, so don't write me hate letters). All these dead players from the past show up and play baseball on this field built in the cornfield.

But in the end, one of those young baseball players turns out to be Ray's father. And Ray sees his father when his father was a young man. And at the close of the movie, the father and son reconnect by throwing the ball together. I showed the clip and listen, it was one of the most touching services I have ever been a part of. It poignantly demonstrates God's desire to spend time with us — like a father and child.

Miracle. In a message on unity and alignment in the church, one of our pastors, Eric Geiger, showed a video clip of the movie *Miracle*. The movie captures the magic and wonder of the 1980 United States Olympic hockey team. Who can forget Al Michaels's famous line, "Do you believe in miracles? Yes!"

As you probably know, the team was an underdog going into the Olympics that year. Their coach, however, was determined to turn that image around and make winners out of this team. He knew this would never happen, however, unless they could learn to play as one. The individual players came from all over the United States, and they all came with different approaches, methodologies, and philosophies to ice hockey. Unless they aligned their energies to a unified strategy, they would never take home a medal.

A clip from the movie shows how the coach created a sense of oneness and alignment of energy. Slip into the movie scene: The coach asked each player who they were and who they played for. Unfortunately, each player gave his name and the college for which he had played. That was not the answer the coach was looking for. Each time the players gave the wrong answer, the coach made them perform skate drills. The drills went on into the night because the team was not giving the right answer. Their answers demonstrated individualism, not team work.

Finally, Mike Eruzione gave the answer everyone needed to hear. He said. "Mike Eruzione, United States of America." Then each player followed his example with the same answer. They stated their name and then followed with "The United States of America." The coach was looking to strip each player of his individual pride and unite the team under one great banner, "The United States of America." Because of the alignment of minds, the team went on to win the gold metal in the Olympics.

The impact of that video clip on our congregation was priceless! It caused us to realize that we had to function as a team if we were going to win our city to Christ. We could not engage in individual turf wars, individual power struggles, and individual agendas. We were going to have to come together as a team to defeat the enemy. The video was verbal and visual and the impact was unforgettable.

Using Drama

Drama is without a doubt one of the most powerful forms of biblical communication. In terms of emotional impact, the acting out of biblical truths enables the audience to see how the Word of God fleshes out in the realities of life. Drama takes the truths of God's Word and visually applies them to the context in which our congregations live.

Having said this, I have to say that drama is also the trickiest of all multisensory teaching tools. It requires training, sequencing, rehearsals, and so on. I am not going to pretend to be an expert here. There is, however, plenty of training available at specialized conferences. I do think that the grid REEKS can tell you if you are ready to use drama.

R: The drama has to be *relevant* to the message. I have witnessed drama in churches and had no clue as to how it connected to the message. This comes across as using drama just to be trendy. "If it doesn't fit, you have to quit."

E. Make sure the performance demonstrates *excellence*. Suffice it to say, this will require practice and rehearsals. Drama that is done right demands time and hard work. Before you launch a sermon that uses drama, make sure you have the quality to pull it off.

E. The drama has to be *engaging*. In other words, it has to be executed in a form that attracts attention. I have personally sat through dramas that were boring and literally served to disengage the audience. Have discerning eyes, evaluate your drama. Make sure your design team looks at it carefully.

K. Seek to be *creative* with your dramatic performances. Look for ways that are unique and fresh to the audience.

S. The drama has to be *seamless* to the flow of the message. This means you need to know how you will verbally transition from the message to the drama and from the drama back to the message, using verbal sentences such as: "Now, with that visual in mind, look at what the Bible has to say." My point is this: Don't be unprepared for those transitions. If not executed with excellence, they can make things seem awkward.

LET THE PEOPLE PARTICIPATE

The first sentence of chapter 1 of this book is an interactive question. Along with the visual at the top of the next page it was designed to suck you into this book. It was designed to make this book a two-way street instead of a one-way street. It was strategically framed to make this book seem like a conversation rather than a lecture. The statement simply read: "Do you consider yourself a *good* communicator or a *great* communicator? If you consider yourself a *good* communicator, would you like to elevate to *great*? If you are already a *great* communicator, would you like to raise the bar to *phenomenal*? You can! And *relax!*—it's not going to complicate your life."

Those interactive questions were not random. They were intentionally engineered to incite an answer in your mind and to engage your interest in the rest of the book. Hopefully, the question forced an honest evaluation in your mind. As I framed that interactive question, I could already picture you standing there in the bookstore pondering the answer. Mind engaged, wondering if this book could help and opening your wallet to see if you have the cash on hand to purchase it. That is the effect of interactive teaching. It draws the learner into the learning process.

But that raises the question: How do we transform our communication from a one-way street into a two-way interactive street? It's not that difficult to do. Here are some practical ways to make your message interactive:

1. Provide a listening guide and ask people to fill in the blanks as you teach. This forces them to pay attention lest they miss the answers to the blank spaces. Often after I teach people will approach me and ask what was the answer to a particular question.

2. Give the audience an interactive element. During a message on prayer, I wanted to drive home the point that the power of prayer lies not in the person offering the prayer but in the God receiving it. The power is not in our faith; the power is in God's faithfulness.

To illustrate this I told about the space probe Voyager 1. Launched years ago, it is currently leaving the farthest outpost of our solar system. In fact I called NASA, and I was told that it had drifted below the elliptical plane of the solar system and was about four billion miles from earth. Incredibly, at that time NASA was still receiving communication signals from the probe.

The signal being emitted from the probe is less energy than is emitted by a penlight, but NASA is able to receive it. You may ask, How can they receive such a weak signal? The answer is simple. Located in Houston, Texas, is an enormous satellite receiver. (I had a huge satellite dish on the stage). It is so powerful that it can detect the weak signal of the probe, weaker than a penlight, at over four billion miles away.

What a picture of our prayers. Your prayers may be weak, like the penlight signal of the probe, but God is powerful and receives your prayers clearly. To make this truth interactive, we gave everyone in the auditorium a penlight. We turned off all the lights in the house and had everyone click on their penlights at once. It made a powerful statement about God's faithfulness to receive our prayers.

In addition, the penlight was designed to be hooked on a key chain. I still see them to this day on people's key chains. It is there to remind them that God always hears their prayers.

3. Give out take-home elements. One of the most effective methods of ensuring continued interaction with the message is to give a take-home element. When we did the series on "The Pursuit of Happiness," we gave out a key chain attachment for each of the beatitudes. We have given out wristbands, bolts, penlights, and other take-home elements that keep the audience interacting with the message long after it is over.

DISCUSSION QUESTIONS

1. Describe the lighting in your teaching and worship environment. How could you make it more multisensory?

2. Describe the sound quality in your teaching and worship environment. How could you make it more multisensory?

3. Discuss how to tune verbal illustrations into multisensory illustrations. Try to come up with an example.

PREACHING A MULTISENSORY MESSAGE

In the third and final part of this book, I want to provide some personal examples of multisensory sermons I have delivered to the congregation at Christ Fellowship. Bear in mind that there are other Christian leaders teaching in a multisensory format, and you can certainly learn from them. Many of them are far more gifted and far more creative than I am, and I hope you will seek them out.

One factor that may set the following messages apart is that they are expositional in nature. I hope you can see how simple it is to transform a lecture exposition into a multisensory exposition. We will look at the use of multisensory teaching from the three "benchmarks" of effective teaching:

1. Attention: Make sure *you* get it.
2. Comprehension: Make sure *they* get it.
3. Retention: Make sure they never *forget* it.

I will give sermon examples showing how to use various multisensory teaching techniques. Put another way: We will give examples of how to make your teaching compelling, crystal clear, and unforgettable. One more bit of information: Three levels of multisensory sermons will be presented in the following categories:

1. *Simple*: an example of a multisensory sermon that is simple to design and simple to execute
2. *Intermediate*: a bit more complex multisensory sermon that may require more time and resources to pull off
3. *Advanced*: a far more complex multisensory sermon that will require human resources, technical resources, and probably financial resources

By looking over these sermons, you should be able to get an idea of how simple this can be and how complicated it can be. The good news is that you can move at your own pace. Each sermon will list the multisensory illustration(s) along with the materials, technical resources, and human resources needed to carry out the message.

ATTENTION: MAKE SURE *YOU* GET IT

But blessed are your eyes because they see, and your ears because they hear.

JESUS

The *launch* of anything is critical — whether you are talking about the launch of a business, the launch of a career, the launch of the space shuttle, or the launch of your message.

The most crucial moments in a space shuttle mission are during the launch sequence. Failure is not an option! For that reason, almost all the fuel is spent in the first eight minutes, just to get the shuttle into orbit. In fact, the engines consume half a ton of fuel every second during the trip to space. NASA has fueled the shuttle with the most powerful fuels known to humankind. No amount of money is spared, no amount of fuel is "too much fuel," and no kind of fuel is considered too powerful.

The investment in terms of time, resources, and energy by NASA at liftoff is staggering. So is the effect. After a successful launch, most of the energy is spent. Because of the momentum created during launch, however, the shuttle can cruise freely in space for an unlimited amount of time.

LAUNCHING YOUR MESSAGE: 3 – 2 – 1 — SERMON LIFTOFF

What a vivid picture of launching your teaching! In the first five minutes, your message either flies or it crashes and burns. It's that simple. It is here, at the introduction, that your message must grab attention and hold it. It is here, at the sermon liftoff, that you achieve critical attention levels, or your message blows up in your face.

Since those first few minutes are so crucial, doesn't it make sense to pour extra energy, extra time, and extra resources into that critical part of the message? In my own personal sermon preparation, I spend an entire morning thinking through the launch sequence of my upcoming message. It is also in these critical launch moments that I spend most of my multisensory energy.

Almost every message I launch begins with highly visual elements and sometimes highly interactive elements. I have found that if the introduction is powerful and captivating, the energy it generates at liftoff will provide the momentum to propel the sermon through the rest of the delivery.

Though I spent a lot of time thinking through each portion of this book, the largest amount of time was spent at the introduction. Why? Because I had to come up with a way to grab your attention. I knew if I didn't grab your attention at the launch of this book, it wouldn't matter how good the rest of it was; you would not read it. The introduction had to be compelling, or you would not invest your time.

With that reality in mind, I pictured you browsing through the bookstore. I tried to imagine the other books that would compete for your attention. I thought about what it would take to grab your initial attention. That would be the cover and the title. It is true: most of us initially judge a book by its cover and by its title. We have to. We can't read the entire book before we buy it.

Next I thought through the beginning part of this book. Why? Because here I would be presenting some of the content, which would either spark your interest or defuse it. I needed a kind of communication that would literally take your attention hostage. Translation: I needed visual images at the beginning. Remember this visual image?

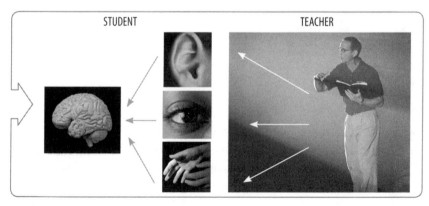

ATTENTION: MAKE SURE *YOU* GET IT   149

The intent was to use every technique in the communication arsenal to compel you to purchase the book. That is precisely the concept I am trying to convey here. Your introduction *cannot* fail.

The following are examples showing how to use various multisensory teaching techniques in order to capture attention. In each case the multisensory communication was presented at the introduction of the message.

SERMON 1: "BAPTISM"

Level: Simple
Sermon Series: Baptism
Sermon Title: Baptism: Your Public Display of Love
Sermon Text: Acts 2:41
Goal of Multisensory Illustration: to gain audience attention quickly and hold onto it.

Resources Needed:

Materials: None
Technical Resources: None
Human Resources:
1. Newlyweds in full wedding attire
2. Wedding march music

Who Needs to Be "In the Know"?

Ushers
Technical crews

Manuscript: As Spoken

Hey everybody, we're going to talk about baptism today, and hopefully have some fun as well as bringing clarity to what baptism is all about. And to do that, I want to create a visual image in your mind, which I hope you'll never forget. I've asked Jordan Caldwell to join me on the stage today. [*Jordan walks on stage dressed in his black wedding tuxedo.*] In case you didn't know, Jordan just got married a few weeks back. I actually got to attend his wedding ceremony, and oh was it beautiful! Jordan is wearing his wedding ceremony garb for us today, in order to help me with the visual image that I want to create in your mind.

I think it goes without saying, there are few ceremonies any more beautiful than a wedding ceremony. In fact, I was thinking back on the sights and sounds of Jordan's wedding. There was the sight of all the flowers, ribbons, and candelabras. There was the large crowd of friends and family gathered in the auditorium for the celebration. There were young men dressed in tuxedos. There were ushers, groomsmen, and the best man. There were beautiful bridesmaids and the maid of honor. And then there was Jordan—the man, the legend, the groom ... standing at the front of the chapel with all the wedding party looking so sharp...

But folks, the crowning jewel of any wedding is ... the bride [*and down the aisle came Julie ... To the utter shock of our congregation, the wedding march begins to play, the auditorium doors open, and Julie comes down the aisle in full wedding garb escorted by her father. The congregation of Christ Fellowship stands as she comes down. She comes to the front of the auditorium and is joined by Jordan and myself. I say to her:*] Julie, you look as beautiful today as you did on your wedding day. Thanks for helping me today.

[*Then I speak to the congregation:*] Mark it, folks: A wedding ceremony is an event they will never forget. Large or small, a wedding ceremony is like magic! But having said that, you realize that the *public* ceremony is not *necessary*. You ask, "What do you mean, it is not necessary?" I simply mean the public ceremony is not necessary for a couple to be legally married. In fact, they can be legally married just by doing two very simple things: Number 1. Say, "I do" before a legal official. Number 2. Do the legal paper work. That's all that's necessary. The *public* ceremony is not necessary.

So why then do couples go through all the preparation of a public wedding ceremony? Why not have a private wedding—just the bride and groom and the legal official? Why go public? The answer is basic: By having a public wedding, the couple makes their love for each other *public knowledge*. By having a public ceremony, the couple is saying, "We want people to *know* that we love each other. We want people to *know* that we are devoted to each other."

Do they *have* to have a public ceremony? Of course not! But don't miss this point: The public ceremony is designed to be a public declaration. The groom is saying, "I want the world to know I love her." The bride is saying, "I want the world to know I love him."

[*I ask Julie, who is standing before me at the front of the church:*] Julie, why go public with your wedding?

[*Julie responds:*] Because I want the world to know I love Jordan.

[*Next, I ask Jordan:*] Jordan, why did you go public with the wedding?

[*Jordan responds:*] Because I want the world to know I love Julie.

Jordan, you may kiss your bride, again. [*Jordan and Julie march out to the wedding music. The crowd applauds loudly. The moment was unforgettable for all who were there.*]

[*I return to talking to the audience:*] Now, let me turn a corner and draw analogy between a *wedding ceremony* and a *baptism ceremony*, because they are a lot alike.

Proposition: Your baptism is designed by God to be like a wedding ceremony between you and the Lord Jesus. Mark it: When you get baptized, it is a *public declaration* of your love for Christ. You are saying publicly: "I want the world to know I love Jesus. I want the world to know I am devoted to him. I want the world to know he has saved me." Mind you, baptism is not what saves us, but it is a public declaration that we have been saved.

How so?

[*Transitional statement:*] Let's find out as we look at God's Word:

[I. Christ Proposes to Us]

Revelation 3:20: "Here I am! I stand at the door and knock. If anyone hears my voice and opens the door, I will come in and eat with him, and he with me." I love that verse! Jesus depicts himself as standing outside the door of our life, and he is knocking at the door of our heart. And the idea is he wants us to open that door and let him into our lives.

Mind you, many people sense God knocking at the door of their heart, but they are afraid to let him in, because they fear what he may want to do with their life. But Jesus says, "If you open the door to your heart, I only want to come in and eat with you."

Andy Stanley says, "There are no more intimate words that Jesus could tag onto the end of this verse than to say, 'I will eat with you and you with me.'" In those days, when someone invited you to eat with him or her, the primary goal was not to consume food. The primary goal was to spend time together, and that is Jesus' goal when he knocks at the door of your heart. And don't miss this truth: Jesus refers to those who open the door as "his bride." In other words, Jesus depicts himself as a groom asking for our hand in marriage, and when we open that door to our heart, we become the bride of Christ. In John 3:29, Jesus says this about us: "The bride belongs to the bridegroom." We belong to him.

The whole connection between God and us is all about a relationship. It's not about religion; it is about a relationship. Jesus asks for our hand in a marriage relationship. Take a look at Jordan asking for Julie's hand. [*Jordan actually asked Julie to marry him while serving in one of our children's ministries. The proposal was caught on tape as he got down on one knee before Julie and in front of all the children. The tape shows all the children clapping and Julie smiling from ear to ear! After the tape was shown to the congregation, there was not a dry eye in the audience.*] That's how God comes to us. He asks us to enter into an eternal relationship with him.

[II. Saying, "I Do" Makes It *Official*]

What I am about to say is critical, so don't miss it. When you invite Christ into your heart, it is synonymous with saying "I do" in a marriage. And when you say "I do" to Christ's proposal, it is legal and official. You don't need a pastor present. You don't need to be in a church. You don't need to be baptized. Just asking Christ into your life eternally secures your salvation. That part of it is personal. It's really between you and God alone! Romans 10:13 says, "Everyone who calls on the name of the Lord will be saved."

[III. Baptism Makes It *Public*]

Acts 2:41 says, "Those who accepted his message were baptized." Don't miss the sequence: Becoming a Christian begins when you accept the message. That is when the relationship begins, when you accept the proposal. The beautiful part of all that is this: Baptism makes your relationship to Christ public knowledge.

"Those who accepted his message were baptized." I love it! Our baptism is like having a public wedding ceremony. Do you have to be baptized to be a Christian? Technically—No! It's like asking, "Do we have to have a public ceremony to be married?" No! Having the ceremony, however, makes your love for one another public knowledge. It's a visual display of your love for one another. That's what baptism is between Jesus and us. It's a visual display of our immersion into Jesus. One more thing: God wants this ceremony carried out in a specific way. Isn't the way a wedding ceremony is conducted important to the bride and groom? Of course it is! It's extremely important. And so it is with God and us. There are three factors that God wants us to get right as we think about our baptism ceremony.

1. Baptism is exclusively for those who have *committed* themselves to Christ.

"Those who accepted his message were baptized." There is exclusiveness to those words. Only those who accept the message are to be baptized. The word "accepted" translates the Greek word *apodechomai*. The word means to reach out and take hold of something; to embrace it as your own; to commit. In other words, the baptism ceremony is exclusively for those who have made a commitment to Christ. Just like a wedding is exclusively for folks who've committed to each other; just like a wedding is exclusively for people who have embraced each other as lovers, in the very same way, the baptism ceremony is exclusively for those who have committed themselves to Christ. The baptism ceremony is exclusively for those who love him.

Ladies, if a guy came to you and said, "Hey, let's have a wedding ceremony, because it looks so cool. But I don't want to be committed to you." You would say to that guy something like, "You are out of your mind." A ceremony without a commitment to one another makes a mockery of the ceremony.

2. Baptism occurs *after* you commit to Christ ... not before.

"Those who accepted his message were baptized." Do you see the sequence? We first commit to Christ, and then we have the baptismal ceremony. Stated another way: We have the wedding ceremony after we say "I do" to Christ, not before. You don't say to someone: "Let's have a wedding ceremony, and after the ceremony, we will decide if we love each other." No way! The commitment comes first. In the same way, you make a commitment to Christ first, and then you have the baptism ceremony.

By the way, this is why baptizing babies makes no sense. A baby has made no commitment to Christ. A baby cannot decide to follow Christ. So, why then do many religions baptize infants? Well, a lot of people, especially in our Miami area, imagine that there are some magical powers in the baptism waters, and by baptizing a baby you essentially inoculate it from judgment.[1] But there is nothing magical in these waters. They come from Miami-Dade water and sewage!

3. Baptism is an act of total *immersion*.

"Those who accepted his message were baptized." Let me repeat the question: "Is the way a wedding ceremony is conducted important to the bride and groom?" It most certainly is! The same is true with our Lord, and here is a crucial part of the ceremony. The whole idea of baptism is to depict *total immersion* into Christ. Have you ever heard someone say, "He is totally immersed in that"? That is the idea of baptism.

Follow me here: The word "baptism" is a translation of the Greek word *baptizo*, which literally means "to immerse something." The translators, unfortunately, did not translate the word, but rather, they transliterated it. In other words, they just slid the Greek *baptizo* over into the English with no meaning given to it.

In reality, however, the word means "to immerse" or "to dunk." For example, the word is used of dipping garments in a dye so as to totally color them. It is the idea of being totally immersed. That is the picture baptism is designed to capture.

When we are immersed, it shows that we are not partially committed to Christ; we are totally immersed in him. That is what makes the whole ceremony so meaningful both to us and to our Lord. We are saying publicly: "We are totally immersed in our Lord."

Now I know some are saying, "Well, I was sprinkled after I was saved ... did that count?" Listen: God always looks at the heart more than the ceremony. If you were sprinkled and your heart was overwhelmed with love for Jesus; then you better know he loved that! Here is the point, however: If Christ who died for you is so immersed in his love for you that he was willing to die for you, don't you know it would be a blessing to him to say: "Jesus, I want to do this again, and I want to do it like you want it?" [*Following this message, 189 people at Christ Fellowship followed Christ in baptism. Many trusted Christ after the message.*]

Multisensory Effect:

Walking onto the stage with the groom dressed in full wedding attire quickly grabbed everyone's attention. The picture of the public wedding ceremony not only grabbed attention, but many people said it clarified two issues for them: (1) Jesus actually wants to have a relationship with us, and (2) baptism is the public ceremony.

SERMON 2: "THE INDISPUTABLE PROOF OF CHRISTIANITY"

Level: Intermediate

Sermon Series: CSI Miami

Sermon Title: The Indisputable Proof of Christianity

Sermon Text: Hebrews 2:1–4

Goal of Multisensory Illustration: To grab attention and to help clarify the theological evidence that proves the truth of Christianity.

Resources Needed

Materials: Set stage like a courtroom: judge's desk and flags on stage platform

Podiums on floor for prosecution and defense attorneys

Technical Resources: Music played over sound system to Perry Mason theme

Human Resources:

1. Judge
2. Bailiff
3. Prosecution: Santana, i.e., Satan the accuser
4. Defense: played by Pastor
5. Jury: played by the congregation

Who Needs to Be "In the Know"?

Ushers

Technical crews

Introduction

Pastor and Santana walk down the aisle at the beginning of message. Both are dressed in suit and tie and carry briefcases to present the idea of a legal trial. As they enter, the music to Perry Mason plays over the sound system. At the same time, the judge and bailiff emerge from the side and take center stage. The judge takes her seat on the platform to begin the trial. The trial begins as the bailiff, played by worship leader, reads the text of the message: Hebrews 2:1 – 4.

Manuscript: As Spoken

Bailiff: Court is called to order this morning. The Honorable Judge Green is presiding. The case at hand: "Unbelief vs. Christianity."

Judge [*played by the Honorable Judge Greene, Miami-Dade County*]: Good morning Dr. Blackwood and Mr. Santana. Mr. Santana, as prosecution, you may proceed with your opening statement.

Prosecution, Mr. Santana [*Santana, played by a young man in the church, steps to the lectern on the lower level and begins his prosecution of the Christian faith*]: Thank you, Your Honor. Your Honor, I'd like to move that we dismiss this case due to the unproven claims of Christianity. Your Honor, *you* know, *I* know, and *the good people* of this jury know that Christianity is just like all other religions out there. It is based purely on emotions. There's not one shred of evidence to support it. It is a blind faith. Your Honor, since there is no evidence to prove the truth of Christianity, I move for a dismissal.

Judge Green: Thank you for those pearls of wisdom, Mr. Santana, but I'm the judge in this courtroom, and as such, I'll make that decision. Dr. Blackwood, you may make your opening statement.

Defense attorney [*played by Pastor Blackwood. Pastor steps to his lectern and begins his public defense of the Christian faith. Santana, the prosecution takes a seat, and the sermon begins here as the pastor presents the incredible evidence that gives indisputable proof for the Christian faith*]: Thank you, Your Honor. Members of the jury, the prosecution would have you believe that the Christian faith is a mindless, thoughtless, unintelligent, blind faith. He'd have you imagine that Christianity is based purely on emotion, that it's devoid of evidence and devoid of substance, and that it's bankrupt of proof. But as usual, Mr. Santana is simply not telling the truth.

Mind you, there are thousands of religions out there, all claiming to be the one true faith. And Mr. Santana is right. None of them present evidence. None of them offer proof to validate those claims. They all call people to blind faith—to faith with no evidence. You have to *hope* it is true, and *hope* you have banked your soul on the right faith.

But Christianity is different! Christianity calls people to faith built on evidence. Christianity is not faith based on emotionalism. It is faith built on intellectual proof and solid evidence. Mark me here, members of the jury: God does not want to bypass your brain and go for your emotions. In fact, God starts with your brain. God stacks up the proof about Jesus. God stacks up the evidence and calls you to *think*. Then, based on a thoughtful consideration of the evidence, he calls you to render your verdict.

Members of the jury: You've been called to render a verdict about the Christian faith. As a public defender of the faith, my goal today is painstakingly simple. I simply want to stack up the evidence that proves that Jesus is the Christ. Then, based on that evidence, you cast the verdict—truth or lie.

By the way: What Mr. Santana doesn't want you to know is that the eternal destiny of your soul depends on the verdict. That's right: You, the jury, are on trial. Eternal life and eternal death are at stake.

Now let me turn a corner and say this: I have deliberately set the mood of a "trial" today for this reason: We're studying the book of Hebrews on the weekends at Christ Fellowship, and the text of chapter 2:4 is written in legal-trial terminology. In this text, God stacks up the evidence like a defense lawyer in order to prove that Jesus is the one true Savior.

Proposition: Christianity is a faith based on a foundation of evidence and substance. It is not based on feelings and emotionalism. It has a solid base of evidence underneath.

Hebrews 11:1 in the King James Version states the basis of the Christian faith: "Now faith is the *substance* of things hoped for, the *evidence* of things not seen." Mark it: The Christian faith is not a call to blind faith. It is a faith built on substance and evidence. By the way: Both of those words, *substance* and *evidence*, have trial law connotations.

For example: The word *substance* is the compound Greek word *hupostasis*. The prefix *hupo* means "under"; *stasis* means "something standing." *Hupostasis*, then, means "something standing under, something substantial"—that is, something that can help substantiate a truth.

The word *evidence* comes from the Greek word *elenchos*, which denotes "the act of presenting evidence for the truth of something."[2] That is the purpose of the book of Hebrews: God stacks up the evidence so that you will be intellectually persuaded.

Interrogator: Rick, there are so many faiths out there, so how do we *know* Jesus is the true Christ?

Transitional statement: Let's find out as we make our way through this text.

[I. The Testimony of God]
Hebrews 2:1–3: "We must pay more careful attention, therefore, to what we have heard, so that we do not drift away. For if the message spoken by angels was binding, and every violation and disobedience received its just punishment, how shall we escape if we ignore such a great salvation?"

The Bible is a book about the salvation of people. The word *salvation* literally means "to save or to rescue." That is the whole drama of redemption. Jesus came to the earth and died on a cross to save us from eternal destruction. Those who embrace that message will be saved, right?

But here is the dilemma: There are thousands of other faiths that make that same claim. There have been thousands of people who have claimed to be the Messiah. How, then, do we know that Jesus is the true Messiah? How can we be certain?

Listen: There is only one way you can be certain about anything. Evidence! Without evidence, you may have faith in something, but you don't know that it is true. God knows that, and God steps forward to give his testimony and to present evidence:

Hebrews 2:4: "God also testified to it." The word *testified* translates the Greek word *martureo*. *Martureo* refers to the legal testimony of a witness. This is explicit! God himself comes to the witness stand to testify to the truth of the gospel. Look back in your Bible to Acts 2:22: "Men of Israel, listen to this: Jesus of Nazareth was a man *accredited* by God."

Again, God steps forward to accredit the validity of Jesus. But, this text tells us *how* God accredits the truth of Jesus. "Men of Israel, listen to this: Jesus of Nazareth was a man accredited by God." The word *accredited* is a graphic word in the Greek text. It translates the compound Greek word *apodeiknumi*. The prefix *apo* denotes the separation of two things. This goes over here, and that over there. *Deiknumi* means "to show, establish truth." *Apodeiknumi*, then, means: "To establish the truth of something by putting space between truth and lie." That's what a trial attorney does. He or she establishes truth by separating the true from the false. The truth goes over here—and the lie goes over there.

That's exactly what God does in the Bible. He validates the truth of the gospel by putting a space between Jesus and all the false messiahs by putting space between Christianity and all the other false religions. And how does God do this? Evidence! Hard Facts!

[II. The Testimony of Evidence]

Acts 2:22: "Men of Israel, listen to this: Jesus of Nazareth was a man accredited by God." How? "By miracles, wonders and signs, which God did among you through him." Get it? The evidence lies in three factors: miracles, wonders, and signs. Go back to Hebrews 2:4, where we read that God also testified to his salvation, how? "by signs, wonders and various miracles." God presents evidence like exhibits A-B-C:

Exhibit A is—signs.
Exhibit B is—wonders.
Exhibit C is—miracles.

Today, we're going to look at exhibit A. The *signs* that prove Jesus is the true Messiah. The word "signs" (*semeia* in Greek) has to do with the fulfillment of prophecy. Let me explain: Throughout the Old Testament, God gave the promise that a Savior would come, a Messiah who would save the world from sin. Those who recognized him and embraced him would be saved.

One problem: As God gave that promise of the coming Savior, Satan flooded the world with false messiahs, making it difficult to be certain of the true Messiah. So how can we know for certain? The answer is in predictive prophecy. God made the decision "foolproof" through predictive prophecy:

Put your thinking caps on. In the Old Testament, written hundreds and thousands of years before Jesus came, God gave a system of 331 prophecies about the coming Messiah. The prophecies foretold detailed things about his life: the time of his arrival, the place of his birth, his ancestors, how he would die, and so on.

The key is this: Only the true Messiah would be able to fulfill all 331 prophecies, thus proving without question that he is the Messiah. Mark it down: Jesus fulfilled all 331 of those verbal predictive prophecies, and God enters these prophecies as evidence. God stacks his case 331 fulfilled prophecies high.

Let's take a look at a few of those prophecies and how Jesus fulfilled them to the letter. Look first to Daniel 9. Let me set this up: This is a predictive prophesy about the first coming of Jesus. It was written over five hundred years prior to Jesus' birth, but it makes a prediction that is staggering.

Daniel 9:25: "Know and understand this [that's like saying, 'be sure you get this']: From the issuing of the *decree* to restore and rebuild Jerusalem." Daniel just marked a day! He just marked a starting point for this prophecy. The starting point in this prophecy is "the day the decree was given to restore and rebuild Jerusalem." You ask, "What day was that?" The answer is March 14, 445 BC. That is the day that Artaxerxes issued the decree to restore and rebuild Jerusalem. That day is marked in history books.

Now, follow the sequence: Marking that day [March 14, 445 BC] as the starting point, "Know and understand this: From the issuing of the decree to restore and rebuild Jerusalem until the Anointed One, the ruler, comes..." [*Stop there*]. Do you realize what Daniel is about to do here? He's about to foretell the time when the Messiah will come. Get the picture: Daniel is standing in the 500 BC era, but he is about to foretell the exact date that the Messiah would first come.

"Know and understand this: From the issuing of the decree to restore and rebuild Jerusalem [March 14, 445 BC] until the Anointed One, the ruler, comes there will be seven 'sevens,' and sixty-two 'sevens.'" Add all that up, and you get sixty-nine "sevens." Put your math caps on. The word "sevens" has to do with "seven-year periods of time." And how many seven-year periods are there? Sixty-nine in this prophecy. So 69 times 7 years adds up to how many years? 483 Jewish years or 173,880 days.

Get it? Daniel says: If you start on March 14, 445 BC, and you go 483 Jewish years into the future, that will be the date that the Messiah will come. Well, folks, if you start on March 14, 445 BC, and you go 483 years into the future (173,880 days), you come to April 6, AD 32. You ask, "What is so significant about that day?" That's the exact day that Jesus rode into Jerusalem and officially presented himself as the Messiah, that is, Palm Sunday.

Get the picture? Daniel 9 predicted the very day that the true Messiah would arrive. Not an approximate date, but an exact date. April 6, AD 32. Jesus perfectly and accurately intersected with that day. By the way, any "would-be Messiah" not around on April 6 32 AD is disqualified—right? Do you see how this narrows the field? That's just one prophecy. There are 331. [*Pastor enters "April 6, AD 32" on a place card as evidence number 1 of exhibit A.*]

Let's examine the prophecy of Psalm 22. Psalm 22 was written one thousand years before Jesus was born, and in this prophecy the psalmist predicts the exact method by which Jesus would be put to death. Psalm

22 is a meticulous description of death by crucifixion. Scripture presents an explicit description of: (1) the piercing of the hands and feet, (2) the dislocation of the joints, (3) the dehydration and shock, (4) and the gambling for garments, which was typical of Roman soldiers during crucifixion.

What is so incredible about that prophecy is this: Crucifixion was not even invented in 1000 BC. Crucifixion was not invented until around 400 BC by the Persians, and was then picked up in 150 BC by Romans and used to crucify Jesus in AD 32. Yet, Scripture accurately describes and foretells the manner in which Jesus would be put to death, and as the true Messiah, Jesus fulfilled that prophecy to the letter.

Get it? Any "would-be Messiah" not around on April 6, AD 32, and who didn't die by crucifixion is disqualified. [*Pastor enters "Crucifixion" on a place card as evidence number 2 of exhibit A.*]

Think of the next prophecy: Have you ever wondered why the New Testament opens with a long list of genealogies? The genealogy traces the ancestry of Jesus back to David and back to Abraham. The reason for that is basic: A thousand years before Jesus came as the Messiah, the Bible predicted that when the true Messiah came, he would be able to trace his lineage back to David and back to Abraham. Jesus was born of that royal lineage and is thus qualified to be the true Messiah. [*Pastor enters "Genealogy" on a place card as evidence number 3 of exhibit A.*]

Don't miss the evidence: Any "would-be Messiah" (1) not around on April 6, AD 32, (2) not put to death by crucifixion, and (3) not born of the lineage of David and Abraham is disqualified as the Messiah. But that's only three prophecies. There are a total of 331 prophecies, and Jesus matched all 331 to the letter.

See how the prophecies lock in the true Messiah? Let me give you a picture: This is a lock. [*Pastor holds up a padlock.*] You know what a lock is. It is made of a series of gears and levers that engage a bolt that swivels on a post and that is pressured by springs. The security the lock provides resides in the fact that only the correctly notched key will match all the levers, gears, and springs and thus have the capacity to turn the bolt. Mind you, the more complex the levers and springs, the more exacting the key has to be to match them.

Now imagine the prophecies of the Old Testament as the complex locking device. God gave 331 explicit detailed prophecies that the true Christ would match.

He would officially declare himself Messiah on April 6, AD 32.
He would ride on a donkey to make that declaration.
He would be put to death by crucifixion.
He would be born of the lineage of David and Abraham.
He would be born in the city of Bethlehem.

There were 331 predictive prophecies that only the true Messiah could match. God so designed this system that it would lock out all the fakes and lock in only the true Messiah. Jesus and only Jesus was able to fulfill all 331 prophecies, proving that he is indeed the Messiah. Listen: You are not left to wonder about Jesus. God did not call you to a blind faith. God has given us solid evidence.

Multisensory Effect

The whole courtroom scene grabbed audience attention at the outset of the message and kept it to the end. The result of presenting the evidence in a trial context gave intellectual credence to the claims of the gospel. The proof really is overwhelming. There were many people saved after this message.

**CHAPTER
11**

COMPREHENSION:
MAKE SURE *THEY* GET IT

*Otherwise they might see with their eyes, hear with their
ears, and understand with their hearts.*

JESUS

Nothing stops sermon momentum like ambiguity. How frustrating for
our audience to come to a service looking for vision and direction only
to be left in confusion and uncertainty. People don't often come back for
that kind of teaching.

Our congregation shows up, waiting for a clear call to action. They are
ready to respond to the vision we cast, the challenge we give, and the text
we proclaim. All they ask for is clarity: "Just make the message clear, so
we can respond to it." If what comes is ambiguous teaching, they are left
paralyzed and frustrated.

The obvious solution is clarity. If ambiguity stops the momentum of
your teaching, clarity keeps it moving. Few teaching methods guarantee
clarity like multisensory teaching. If comprehension is seen as "connecting
the dots," multisensory teaching "puts the dots closer together."

Few passages spell out the disaster we create when we are unclear better than 1 Corinthians 14. In a wonderful message called "The Power of
Clarity," Bill Hybels points out how crucial it is for the pastor-teacher to
be clear.[1] The following analogy of a trumpet blower is derived from that
teaching.

THE CLEAR TRUMPET CALL
Which army perfected the use of trumpets for military warfare? It was
the Roman army. They developed a sophisticated unit of trumpet blowers,
who were trained to blast forty-three different sounds, and each one communicated a different command.

In those days there were no radio communications. So on the battle-field, trumpet sounds were used to communicate specific orders. The commanding officer would dispatch orders to the trumpet blowers. The trumpet blowers would then blow a specific sound that matched that order. Soldiers on the battlefield would hear that sound, and they knew exactly what the commanding officer had ordered them to do.

For example, there was a specific sound that communicated the order to charge into battle. There was an opposite sound that communicated the order to retreat from the battle. But those trumpet sounds had to be distinguishable. They had to be clear and certain.

With those facts in mind, what does the Bible cite as the unpardonable sin of the military trumpet blower? What is the one thing he must never do? The Bible says he must never blow an uncertain sound; he must never blow an unclear sound. Look at 1 Corinthians 14:8: "If the trumpet does not sound a clear call, who will get ready for battle?" That Scripture paints an explicit scenario. Picture ten thousand soldiers marching toward the enemy, but they stop to wait for orders from the commanding officer. The commanding officer, meanwhile, surveys the battlefield to determine if they should attack the enemy or run from the enemy. Finally, he makes his decision. The mission is to charge.

The commanding officer then summons the trumpet blowers together and tells them, "Take your places and give the sound on your trumpet that communicates the order to charge into the battle." Now feel the moment: All ten thousand soldiers are poised for action. They are ready to charge or retreat — whatever the command is. And they wait for that command.

Then, they see the trumpeters line up on the hilltops. They see the trumpeters place the trumpets to their lips. At that moment, here is what the Bible says must never happen. The trumpet blower must not blow an uncertain sound. Can you imagine ten thousand soldiers looking at each other and saying, "What the heck did that mean?" Such a lack of clarity would paralyze the entire army.

Yet, that is precisely what many people in our churches say every weekend. "What the heck did that mean?' They want to do something for God, but often our message is unclear. Lack of clarity is the unpardonable sin of the trumpet blower, and it is the unpardonable sin for pastors and teachers.

What a graphic picture of the duty of the teacher of the Word. As pas-tors and teachers we are God's trumpet blowers. We take the message given to us from the Commander's Word, and we transmit that signal to the troops. God's army stands ready to respond to his Word. The one factor they ask for, however, is *clarity*.

Note 1 Corinthians 14:8 – 9 again: "If the trumpet does not give a *clear call*, who will get ready for battle? So it is with you. Unless you speak intelligible words with your tongue, how will anyone know what you are saying?" The word *intelligible* translates the Greek term *eusemos*, which means "clear ... plain."[2] In other words, the teaching of the pastor must be clear and definite so that no one can mistake the communication.

The research in the first part of this work clearly demonstrates that multisensory communication helps make our teaching clearer. By weaving multisensory communication into our teaching and by creating a multisensory learning environment, we can hold onto our audience's attention and also make things that may be unclear — very clear.

It has been my practice to resort to multisensory techniques, especially when I am tackling issues that might be difficult to comprehend. Verbal communication supported by visuals and interactive teaching can make many theological concepts easier to grasp. The following are examples of sermons in which I used a multisensory teaching technique to help clarify a theological truth.

SERMON 3: "ROPER DOPE"
Level: Intermediate
Sermon Series: The Passion of the Christ
Sermon Title: Roper Dope
Sermon Text: John 18:1 – 11
Goal of Multisensory Illustration: To clarify the theological truth about Jesus' control over his own death.

Resources Needed
Materials:
1. Boxing gloves.
2. One side of a boxing ring on the stage.
3. Pastor has hands taped in boxer style as he walks on stage.
Technical Resources:
1. Video recording of Ali – Foreman fight in Zaire, Africa, and video of earlier Foreman – Frazier fight. Also clips from the movie *The Passion*.
2. Screens to project video or TV placed in smaller auditorium

Who Needs to Be "In the Know"?

Technical crews

Manuscript: As Spoken

I did my share of competitive boxing when I was a kid—my Dad made sure of it. If you know anything about boxing, you know this: If you're fighting a brawler, that is, a heavy puncher, you never—never—let him pin you on the ropes. [*Pastor backs up against ropes as if pinned to the ropes.*] To be "on the ropes" is to be defenseless. To be "on the ropes" is to be helpless. It is to be at the mercy of the one who pinned you there. A boxer, there-fore, would never stay on the ropes intentionally ... or would he?

Slip into this electric scene. [*Video showing the sights and sounds of the crowd gathered to watch the Ali–Forman fight.*] The evening is Octo-ber 30, 1973. The place is Zaire, Africa. The event? The heavyweight championship of the world. The fighters are: George Foreman, a brawler, and Muhammad Ali.

Now, if you know anything about Muhammad Ali, you know he was not a brawler. Ali could throw knock-out punches, but he was not a brawler. He beat his opponents not by brawling with them, but by outsmarting them. He beat them mentally; he beat them strategically; and nowhere did he better demonstrate this than in his battle with George Foreman.

Mind you, Foreman was huge, and he could throw bone-crunching punches. In fact, months before he had knocked Joe Frazier out cold. [*Film showing Foreman knocking out Frazier with devastating power!*] Go-ing into this fight, everyone thought Foreman would do the same to Ali.

But Ali had a plan for Foreman that would take him down. This was the strategy: From the opening bell, Ali backed himself against the ropes. O yeah. Foreman didn't drive Ali into the ropes, but rather, Ali went there of his own will. And, as Ali was on the ropes, Foreman unleashed seven rounds of thunderous blows. [*Film of Foreman pounding Ali as Ali is against the ropes.*]

Had you watched the fight, you might have thought that Ali was at the mercy of Foreman. You might have thought Ali was helpless against this assault. In fact, Ali's corner was shouting to him, "Get off the ropes! Get off the ropes!" Angelo Dundee, his trainer, was screaming for him to get off the ropes! But Ali stayed on the ropes intentionally. You ask, "Why did he stay on the ropes?" The answer is simple: This was the plan; this was the strategy.

For seven rounds, Ali leaned on the ropes and took everything Fore-man could throw. *Until*—Forman had thrown everything he had. And then, to the amazement of everyone, Ali threw a powerful right cross.

[*Film showing Ali taking Forman's punches and then throwing the right cross. The announcer shouts, "Down goes Foreman," and the crowd goes wild with excitement! I return to talking to audience.*] And down went Foreman—in utter defeat! Leaning on the ropes was the plan.

Now, let me turn a corner and bring that scene over to a scene far more sobering. When you read the account of Jesus' crucifixion and when you see the movie *The Passion of Christ*, you might be proned to think Jesus was at the mercy of his killers. You might be proned to think that Jesus was helpless. In fact, as I watched the movie and saw Jesus suffering on the cross, I wanted to say, "Jesus, get off the cross. Call the angels." But understand this: Jesus went to the cross—intentionally! You ask, "Why did he do that?" The answer is simple. This was his strategy to defeat Satan and death.

On the cross,[3] Jesus allowed Satan to unleash all he had. [*Show images from the movie* The Passion, *particulary Christ hanging on the cross.*] For hours, Jesus absorbed the fist beatings, blows with rods, thirty-nine lashes with a flagellum, a crown of thorns, the carrying of a cross to the site of execution, being nailed to the cross. For six hours, Jesus stayed on the cross and took everything Satan could throw. *Until*—Satan had thrown everything he had. And then, to the amazement of all, Jesus rose from the dead and crushed Satan's head forever.

Proposition: When Jesus was suffering on the cross, he was in complete control. Jesus said in John 10:17–18: "I lay down my life—only to take it up again. No one takes it from me, but I lay it down of my own accord." Mark this: From his arrest in the garden to his resurrection, Jesus was in absolute control. He was not at the mercy of Satan. He was not at the mercy of his killers. His death was a calculated plan—a strategy to crush Satan and to rescue us from hell. That truth becomes very clear in the narrative of John 18:1–12.

[I. The Plot at Hand (John 18:1–3)]
"When he had finished praying ..." The King James Version reads here, "When he had finished all these words." What words? All the words from John 13 through 17. Get the picture: Back in chapter 13, Jesus and the twelve had gathered in the upper room for their final meal together. After exposing Judas Iscariot and sending him away into the night, Jesus began to express his love to the remaining eleven. He taught them, encouraged them, and prayed for them. Those words he spoke to them in that upper room are recorded in John 13–17.

As we come to chapter 18, however, we turn a major corner in narrative. "When he had finished praying, Jesus left with his disciples and crossed the Kidron Valley" (the KJV refers to a "brook" here). Stop there and slip into the scene: Jesus and the eleven disciples leave the upper room, walk down the back slopes of Jerusalem down into the Kidron Valley, and they crossed the Brook Kidron.

Historically, that is not without great significance, and let me tell you why. As you well know, it was Passover in Jerusalem at this time. Passover was an annual Jewish ceremony in which millions of Jews flocked into Jerusalem to offer a sacrifice. In fact, one census taken during this time revealed that 3.2 million Jews came to Jerusalem, and they sacrificed 362,000 lambs during the week of Passover!

Picture that scene: All the lambs were killed in the temple, and the blood was dashed on the altar as a sacrifice to God to cover sins. Now folks, as you might imagine, this created a bloody mess in the temple. Lambs blood was flowing at an unimaginable rate, and that raises the question: "How did the Jewish people dispose of all that blood? Where did they send it?"

The answer is quite simple: The Jewish people built a channel down to the little brook in the Kidron Valley. They constructed a trough from the altar down to Brook Kidron, and through that channel the blood of all those lambs was drained away. One historian writes: "The little Brook Kidron literally ran red with blood during Passover."

Now think of it! When Jesus crossed that Kidron Valley, it would have been red with the blood of all those lambs, which had been sacrificed. As Jesus stepped across the brook, he would have seen the blood, and the thought of his own final blood sacrifice would surely have been vivid in his own mind. And as "the Lamb of God," Jesus came to put an end to the entire sacrificial system. Remember, the blood of all those lambs never took away people's sin. It only covered it. Jesus' blood does not cover sin; his blood shed at Calvary removes it once and for all.

Now when we read John 18:1, it has great significance! "When he had finished praying, Jesus left with his disciples and crossed the Kidron Valley. On the other side there was an olive grove, and he and his disciples went into it." Jesus and the eleven crossed the Brook Kidron and then entered a garden.

The garden, of course, is the Garden of Gethsemane. This is the garden where Jesus went to pray and to prepare himself before "all hell" literally broke loose against him. When he had finished praying, verse 2 says, "Now Judas, who betrayed him, knew the place, because Jesus had often met there with his disciples." Judas knew exactly where Jesus would be. He knew Jesus would go to this garden, because this garden was actually his home. Jesus said, "Foxes have holes and birds of the air have nests, but the Son of Man has no place to lay his head" (Matthew 8:20). When evening came and everybody went home to their families and fireplaces, Jesus went to this garden.

So Judas knew where to look. "So Judas came to the grove, guiding a detachment of soldiers and some officials of the chief priests and Pharisees. They were carrying torches, lanterns and weapons." Stop there and get the picture: Judas comes to the garden with a detachment of soldiers. The phrase "detachment of soldiers" translates the Greek word *speira*. A *speira* was a detachment of Roman auxiliary soldiers. Get this: It was comprised of as many as six hundred soldiers.

So Judas came to the grove, guiding six hundred soldiers and some officials from the chief priests and Pharisees. They were carrying torches, lanterns, and weapons. What's up with that? Why would you send six hundred infantry with lanterns, torches, and weapons to arrest one solitary man? I'll tell you why: Many of them had seen him raise the dead! They had seen him give sight to the blind! They had heard of his incredible power! Beyond that, they must have thought Jesus would be hiding in the garden. They imagined they would have to search in the hillside nooks and crannies to overpower him.

But on the contrary, these soldiers are about to be overpowered by Jesus. We've seen the plot at hand. Next notice:

[II. The Power of Jesus (John 18:4–9)]
"Jesus, knowing all that was going to happen to him, went out and asked them, 'Who is it you want?'" Get it: Jesus was not hiding; he was not cringing. No, he stepped forward! He turned tables! They came to confront him, but he confronted them! "Who is it you want?"

"'Jesus of Nazareth,' they replied." (Watch this.) "'I am he,' Jesus said." Put your thinking caps on. If you look at the pronoun "he" in verse 5 in the King James Version, you will notice it is in italics. Meaning what? Meaning it has been added by the translators. In other words, "he" is not in the original Greek text! Jesus did not say "I am he." He simply said, "I am!"

Whose name is "I am?" That's God's name. When Moses stood before God at the burning bush, God said, "[My name is] I AM WHO I AM" (Exodus 3:14). That name reaches back to the preexistence of God! This is the name that carries the power of the Godhead! By the way, who was Jesus? He was God Almighty in the flesh. And the soldiers who came to arrest him were about to be reminded of that fact.

"When Jesus said, 'I am . . .' they drew back and fell to the ground." By the enunciation of his name "I am," six hundred soldiers were knocked down. They went sprawling. They came to overpower Jesus, but he overpowered them.

In a gracious way, he let them know they were not taking him by force. Jesus said: "I lay down my life—only to take it up again. No one takes it from me, but I lay it down of may own accord."

Then verse 7 reads: "Again he asked them, 'Who is it you want?' And they said, 'Jesus of Nazareth.'" You have to wonder about guys ... I mean, they pick themselves up off the ground and parrot the orders "Uh, Jesus of Nazareth." We continue: "'I told you that I am...' Jesus answered. 'If you are looking for me, then let these men go.'" The soldiers came to arrest all twelve, but Jesus made sure his disciples went free. He protected them!

We have seen "The Plot at Hand" and "The Power of Jesus' Word." Now:

[III. The Plan of God (John 18:10–11)]

"Then Simon Peter, who had a sword, drew it..." I love it! Six hundred soldiers, armed to the teeth, and Peter draws his sword on all of them! Talk about guts! But why not? Peter knew the power of the one at his side! He'd seen him raise the dead. He'd seen him walk on water, and he knew what drove the soldiers to their knees. So, he draws his sword! "Then Simon Peter, who had a sword, drew it and struck the high priest's servant, cutting off his right ear. (The servant's name was Malchus.)"

Get the picture? This old warrior, named Malchus, was just doing his job. He had been sent by the high priest to arrest Jesus, and he was just following orders. So he reached out to arrest Jesus, but in a fit of rage, Peter unsheathed this sword and hacked off Malchus's ear.

Imagine the electricity! Peter severs the servant's ear! Malchus touches the place where his ear had been and feels the blood streaming, and immediately six hundred Roman swords ring from scabbards! Now, it goes without saying, things could quickly get out of hand. I love Peter's passion, but it is out of order.

But, watch how Jesus keeps control: "Jesus commanded Peter, 'Put your sword away!'" Luke's gospel shares another incredible element about this moment. In Luke 22:50–51 we read: "And one of them [Peter] struck the servant of the high priest [Malchus], cutting off his right ear. But Jesus answered, 'No more of this!' And he touched the man's ear and healed him." Wow! In complete and majestic control, Jesus says, "Peter, put away your sword." Then, he doesn't reach down and pick up Malchus's old ear and stick it on. No, he just touches the place where it was and gives Malchus a brand new one! How? He is God! Quietly, six hundred Roman swords return to their scabbards. Jesus never loses control! He controls men, events, and history to bring about his own execution.

Just a footnote to this scene: There is a legend that comes to us from early church history (that is, the history of the church shortly after

Christ's death and resurrection). If you look at the names of those who came to faith in Christ after his death and search the annals, there appears the name Malchus—the high priest's servant. This man witnessed the power of the Messiah, and it changed him forever!

"Jesus commanded Peter, 'Put your sword away! Shall I not drink the *cup* the Father has given me?'" (John 18:11). You ask, "What is the cup?" It is the dreadful cup! The cross! Jesus prayed in the garden: "Father, if you are willing, take this *cup* from me; yet not my will, but yours be done." The cup means to be willingly beaten and tortured, and to take on the sins of the world. This is the plan of God. Jesus is saying, "Peter, get out of the way! The Father and I planned this before the foundation of the world. This is the only way you or anyone else can be rescued from hell. I have to do this if you are to be saved."

Isaiah 53:10 reminds us, "Yet it was the Lord's will to crush him and cause him to suffer, and though the Lord makes his life a guilt offering, he will see his offspring and prolong his days." Jesus majestically, omnipotently, and sovereignly controlled and superintended everything so that plan would be executed.

And we worship him today—not as some poor, unfortunate victim. No, we worship his majesty as the "I AM—God Almighty," who shed his blood so that we might live!

Multisensory Effect

This message gave many people a sense of the power and deity of Jesus Christ. They no longer saw him as a victim at the mercy of evil men, but they saw him controlling men, events, and history to bring about our salvation.

SERMON 4: "WHAT IS MAN — PART 3"

Level: Advanced

Sermon Series: What Is Man?

Sermon Title: What Is Man — Part 3

Sermon Text: Hebrews 2:6 – 8

Goal of Multisensory Illustration: To bring clarity to the complicated issues that surround creation and evolution. To answer the question posed by Scripture itself in the text: "What is man?"

Resources Needed

Materials

1. Boat motor on stage. Split in half if possible, with the top off to expose motor, drive shaft, and propeller
2. Video of flagellum motor

Technical Resources: Video
Human Resources: None

Who Needs to Be "In the Know"?

Technical crews to fire film at appropriate time

Manuscript: As Spoken

This is a Yamaha outboard motor. [*Mounted outboard motor on stage.*] You know what an outboard does? It gives a boat the capacity to move through the water. An outboard can propel a boat forward and backward and turn it right or left. This split view reveals the simple mechanics of an outboard unit. [*We placed an outboard on the stage with the covers removed. This exposed the vertical drive shaft as well as the gears and the prop.*] The motor on top rotates a vertical drive shaft, which spins a gear, turns a prop, and propels the boat through the water.

However, a closer look reveals the complexity of an outboard. Within this unit there are hundreds of intricate parts. [*The top cover is off the outboard exposing all the motor's complex parts.*] There are pistons, cams, valves, shafts, bearings, rotors, and a prop. All of these parts are custom made and custom fitted, and they all fire in a precise sequence.

In fact, there's a fascinating law of physics at work in the motor. It is called "the law of irreducible complexity." This law simply means that in order for this motor to operate, three essential factors must be realized. [*Pointing to the motor, the pastor says*]:

1. Every one of these hundreds of parts has to be present within the motor.
2. Every one of these parts has to be in the precise location within the motor.
3. All these parts have to work in an exacting form and fire in precise sequence.

And unless each one of these parts is present, in the precise place, and firing in a precise sequence, the motor will not run. What we see here is incredible complexity!

Incidentally, if I were to ask you: "How did this outboard originate? How did it come into existence?" you wouldn't have to think twice. The order, the arrangement, the complexity tells you someone created this. This didn't evolve out of thin air. This is the product of intelligent design.

Now let me change gears and say this: Did you know that inside your body are billions of microscopic outboard motors far more complex than this one? That's right! Now to show you that, we have to go down into your "molecular self." We're going down past your skin, past the cells, past the bacteria, down into the larger and smaller molecules to find these incredible outboard motors.

Put your thinking cap on tight! The most fundamental units of life are the cells. Cells are the microscopic building blocks of life, and your body is a literal universe of cells. By the way, Charles Darwin, the guy who cracked up the idea of evolution, thought a cell was just a glob of protoplasm, like a little piece of jelly. But in the last century, our knowledge of the human cell has exploded with information!

When we look down into the cell, we see an entire molecular city at work, with machines and engines and information systems. For example, there are "molecular trucks" that carry supplies to the cell. There are machines that capture the energy of sunlight and convert it to usable energy. Stay with me on this:

One of these molecular machines is called "The Bacterial Flagellum." [*Film of flagellum motor on screens in action.*] The bacterial flagellum is a microscopic motor that propels the bacteria through liquid. Just as an outboard motor propels a boat through the water, the bacterial flagellum propels bacteria through the liquid it lives in.

Don't miss this [*microscopic picture of flagellum motor*]. Biochemists use an electron micrograph to magnify the flagella fifty thousand times, and when they look down into this motor, they see incredible complexity. They see a drive shaft, gears, a stator, a rotor, and a propeller. In fact, when you first see this thing you have to think: DANG, that's an outboard motor! That's a Yamaha outboard with complexity.

But get this! The "flagella outboard" has a water-cooled engine. That engine spins at 100,000 rpm, and it is hardwired with sensors that stop and turn it on a dime. And mark it: Just like the boat motor, the *law of irreducible complexity* is at work. In other words, for the flagella motor to work, each of these parts has to be:

1. Present
2. In the right location
3. Firing in a precise sequence

And unless all the parts are present, in the right location, and firing in a precise sequence, the motor doesn't work! *Incredible complexity!*

But the question I want to pose today is one of origin: How did the flagellum motor originate? How did this complex outboard motor get assembled? The larger question is how did *all* of our biological systems originate? The ultimate question of course is: How did man originate? In fact, that is the question of the text (Heb. 2:6): "But there is a place where someone has testified: 'What is man?'"

Folks, there's the most fundamental question of life. What *is* man? Not *who* is man? *What* is man? There are only two possible answers to that question. (1) Man is the product of a Creator. (2) Man is the product of evolution. Here's my proposition today:

Proposition: I want to show you that the theory of evolution is scientifically flawed. In other words, the theory of evolution cannot be supported scientifically. It will not hold water biologically, chemically, or mathematically.

Interrogative: You ask, "Where does evolution violate scientific laws?"

Transitional Statement: Put your thinking caps on even tighter!

[I. The Theory of Evolution]

Verse 6: "But there is a place where someone has testified: 'What is man?'" Stop there. When the question is asked, "What is man? How did man originate?" the evolutionist begins by eliminating God as a possible answer a priori. In other words, before he even begins to consider the issue of origins, the evolutionist eliminates God as a possibility—not on the basis of science, not on the basis of physics, but on the basis of religion!

O yes! Make no mistake; the evolutionist is first and foremost an atheist! He is not a scientist looking for answers, but an atheist out to get rid of God! Francis Crick (Nobel Laureate) and evolutionary biologist writes: "Biologists must constantly keep in mind, that what they see was not designed, but evolved."

Wow, they have to *remind* themselves that it evolved. That is laughable! But you see, before the evolutionist asks the question about the origin of life, he or she rules God out: They rule out Intelligent Design. Folks, no matter how you slice it, that is not scientific research. That is a predisposed agenda. But since the atheist rules God out, evolution is all he has.

Now, let's get down to brass tacks. What is evolution? The theory of evolution as it is now taught basically says, as Ron Carlson, a professor of mine at Grace Theological Seminary, has taught: "Some three to four billion years ago, there was a large inorganic ocean of nitrogen, ammonia salts, methane, and carbon dioxide. The evolutionist says it was bubbling away. Blub blub blub, and then one day—Poof! There arose an amino acid. Then there arose polypeptides. Then there arose protein molecules. And from there the theory of evolution says: Non-living matter rose upward in complexity to form living matter. Then living matter rose upward in complexity to form conscious matter. Then conscious matter rose upward into complexity to become self-conscious matter."

So the theory of evolution assumes the upward progression from chaos to greater and greater organization. Simplicity to greater and greater complexity. From nonliving matter to living matter, and it all happened by chance and natural selection. But, the question is this: Is that scientifically possible? Is evolution based on true science? The answer is "no," for several reasons, and I'm going to focus on two of them.

[II. The Flaws in the Theory of Evolution]
Evolution is scientifically flawed for the following reasons.

(1) The law of biogenesis. You know, and I know, that there are laws of physics that govern our world, such as gravity, entropy, and thermodynamics. There are also laws of chemistry that govern our world, such as matter, chemical compounds, and the like. And there are laws of biology that govern our world. One of the most fundamental laws of biology is *the law of biogenesis*. This law basically states, "Life can only originate from life." Stated another way, "Life cannot originate from nonliving matter. Life cannot evolve from nonliving matter."

Yet, that is exactly what evolution propagandizes—that nonliving matter rose upward in complexity to form living matter. That assumption violates fundamental laws of biology. The entire basis of evolution rests on a biological impossibility, and that is a problem for the evolutionist. But be prepared, because no matter what scientific logic you throw at the evolutionist, he will dream up some wild theory, because for him, it just cannot be God!

He will, therefore, contradict laws of physics, chemistry, and biology, which are the fundamental building blocks of scientific research, and dream up some wild scenario. They have to maintain wild imaginations. But listen, this is one law of science he cannot dream past. Dr. George Wald, professor emeritus of biology at Harvard University (he won the Nobel Prize in biology) wrote this in *Scientific American* on the origin of life: "When it comes to the origin of life, you have only two possibilities as to how life arose. One is spontaneous generation. The other is a supernatural creative act of God. There is no third possibility."[4]

Then he wrote these mind-blowing words: "Spontaneous generation, the idea that life arose from nonliving matter, that idea was scientifically disproved 160 years ago by Louis Pasteur. That leads us scientifically to only one possible conclusion. Life arose as a supernatural creative act of God. But, I will not accept that philosophically, because I do not want to believe in God. Therefore I choose to believe in that which I know is scientifically impossible ... spontaneous generation."

What was Dr. Wald saying? He was saying you only have two choices. (a) Man is the product of God. (b) Man is the product of spontaneous generation, which is impossible!

There is a second reason evolution is scientifically flawed and that is:

(2) The law of irreducible complexity. Let's go back to the flagellum motor. [*Picture on screens.*] Irreducible complexity says that for this motor to operate, every one of these hundreds of parts must be present, in the right place, and functioning in the precise sequence. And unless every one of the parts is present, in the right place, and firing in the right sequence, the motor will not run. Period!

The problem with evolution is that it says the parts of this motor arose gradually over millions and millions of years. You say, "So what?" Well, if spontaneous generation were at work, it would have eliminated any part of that motor that did not operate immediately. So when the tail arose, if it did not immediately advance a cell, if it did not immediately begin moving the bacteria, evolution would have eliminated it. In other words, the only way the motor could be advanced by evolution is if it were completely assembled at once, not by gradual modifications.

But even the evolutionist knows evolution could not have assembled this complex engine out of thin air. Darwin admitted: "If it could be demonstrated that any complex organ existed which could not possibly have been formed by numerous, successive, slight modifications, my theory would break down." It breaks down at every turn, Charles!

The evolutionist imagines that the laws of physics and biology were somehow broken, but he also has to imagine the laws of probability were broken. What do I mean? Just this:

At the Center for Probability Research in Biology, scientists have applied the laws of probability to the possibility of a single cell coming into existence by chance. To give evolution the benefit of the doubt, they computed a world where amino acids bind at a rate one and a half trillion times faster than they do in nature. Even at that rate, however, to get a single cell, the single smallest cell known to mankind—*mycroplasm hominis H 39*—would take 10 to the power of 119,741 years [$10^{119,741}$]. We cannot fathom a number like that, so let me give you a mental picture of it. If I took thin pieces of paper and wrote zeros on them, and I wrote 10 to the power of 119,741, the little zeros would fill the entire known universe. That's how many years it would take to develop one simple cell. By the way, French scientist Emil Borel points out that if anything on the cosmic level exceeds the probability ratio of 10 to the power of 50, it will never happen.

The point is this: What is man? Man is not the product of evolutionary random accidents. Evolution is a twentieth-century religious sect, with no scientific evidence to prop it up. Verse 6 again: "But there is a place where someone has testified: 'What is man that you are mindful of him, the son of man that you care for him?'"

That is a rhetorical question. "God, why are you so mindful of man? Why do you care so much about us?" The answer is verse 7: "You *made* him." Scripture says, "Man is not the outcome of evolution. He is the end result of a creative act of God, and that is precisely why God loves us and cares so much about us.

Multisensory Effect

There were a number of conversions to Christ after this message. I received many anecdotal testimonies, especially from high school and college kids, about how the picture of the outboard made the teaching very clear.

CHAPTER 12

RETENTION:
MAKE SURE THEY NEVER *FORGET* IT

Do you have eyes but fail to see, and ears but fail to hear?
And don't you remember?

JESUS

NASA scientists created a host of brand-new technologies during the race to the moon. Many of them not only helped us reach the moon, but they have since been used in normal, everyday life. One of the substances that NASA scientists engineered was Velcro. This is a two-part substance that enables one item to stick to the other. One side of the Velcro is engineered with thousands of little hooks. The other side is designed to stick to those hooks. It works like a charm.

What a picture of multisensory communication. The verbal, visual, and interactive presentation functions like the hooks on Velcro. When you design a sermon to be multisensory, you are in effect engineering the teaching to stick! The research in this work demonstrates that such a statement is not just words, it is a neurological, theological, and research-based fact.

The following are examples showing how to use various multisensory teaching techniques in order to create long-term memory.

SERMON 5: "HOW TO LIVE AN UNFORGETTABLE LIFE"
Level: Simple
Sermon Series: Matthew
Sermon Title: How to Live an Unforgettable Life
Sermon Text: Matthew 26:6 – 13
Goal of Multisensory Illustration: To create long-term memory

Resources Needed

Materials:

1. Small index size cards. Used to spray perfume on before service begins. Cards will be scented with the perfume "Unforgettable" and given to each audience member as they exit the auditorium. If possible, print the word "Unforgettable" on the front side. On the backside of the card, print the necessary steps for living an unforgettable life.

2. Film. Begin sermon introduction at a cemetery. Film the introduction and show on screens if possible. If there are no video resources, simply talk about death from the pulpit.

Technical Resources: Video
Human Resources: None

Who Needs to Be "In the Know"?

Ushers to hand out scented cards at end of service
Technical crews to fire film at appropriate time

Manuscript: As Spoken

[*Prerecorded talk from the graveyard.*] Hey, everybody, I'm coming to you from the graveyard. Oh yeah! Now, before you all bolt for the door, sit back down and let me explain. Why do we dread the thought of the grave? It's not just that we fear death. Well, that's part of it, but, perhaps even more than that, we fear the thought of being forgotten! Out of sight—out of mind. And the truth is, that is exactly what happens. I hear people promise a deceased loved one at the graveside, "Dad, we will *never* forget you." "Honey, I will *never* forget you." "Friend, I will *always* remember you." They mean that with all their heart, and perhaps they will not forget.

But the fact is: Given enough years, we will be forgotten. Our body gets buried, and so does the memory of our existence. Granted, our children may not forget us. Our grandchildren may remember us. But, given the passage of enough generations, people won't even know we existed, much less remember us.

Ask yourself: "Do you know who your great-great-great-great-grandparents were?" They are buried somewhere, but it's unlikely that you or anyone alive knows who they were, where they are buried, or that they even passed through this world. That's what life comes to. We are forgotten. The atheist Mark Twain lamented this fact when he wrote something like this: "When we die, we vanish from a world, which will weep over us for a day, and then they forget us forever." [*End of video. Back to auditorium—pastor speaks.*]

Did you get that? When we die, people weep for us for a day at the grave, and then they forget us forever. Make no mistake, to be totally forgotten is the inexorable end of all of us. It's as if successive generations have generational amnesia when it comes to remembering our existence. Fact is, no matter how cool we imagine ourselves to be, no matter how important and unforgettable we think we are, we are all very *forgettable*.

You may be saying to yourself: "Thanks, Rick, for the encouraging thoughts. Am I glad I came to church today!" Hold on, because I have great news:

Proposition: God gives to all of us the opportunity to live an *unforgettable life*. God gives us, literally, the once-in-a-lifetime chance to live a life that will outlast our existence.

Interrogative: You ask, "How in the world can I live a life that will never be forgotten? How can I live a life that will be unforgettable?"

Transitional statement: Let's find out as we look at a play-by-play between a woman and the Son of God. There are three actions modeled by this girl that produce an unforgettable life.

Look at Matthew 26:13: "I tell you the truth, wherever this gospel is preached throughout the world, what she has done will also be told, in *memory* of her." Translation? This girl did some things that made her life "unforgettable to God." And by looking at the three actions she took, we discover three actions that produce a life that will be unforgettable by God. Here they are: If you want to live an unforgettable life, it begins when you:

[I. Come to Christ]

"While Jesus was in Bethany in the home of a man known as Simon the Leper, a woman *came* to him." [*Stop there and slip into the moment.*] This woman, whoever she is, walks into this home where Jesus is a guest, and she closes the gap between herself and Christ. This was the *beginning* of her unforgettable life!

Now let me set up the scene: The scene here is the home of Simon. By the way, in only a few hours after this, Jesus will be arrested, tried, and executed. Events after the meal at this house happen rapid-fire and without stopping until Jesus is dead and buried.

But, let me paint the picture of this house for you. To begin with, houses in ancient Israel were constructed around a courtyard. The courtyard would contain a small garden, a fountain, and a table to eat meals. That is precisely the setup of this narrative. Jesus and his little band of disciples have been invited into the home of Simon, and they are gathered around the table eating and no doubt conversing. Their conversation, however, is about to be interrupted! "While Jesus was in Bethany in the home of a man known as Simon the Leper, a woman came to him."

I have to tell you that what this woman did was culturally unacceptable. You see, the ancient Jewish world was not unlike the Taliban world of our day when it came to women. A woman in ancient Jewish culture had no rights politically, and she had no rights socially. Ancient Israel was a male-controlled and male-dominated society, and one of the ways all that trickled down to normal life was this: Women were not permitted to just walk into the presence of men. This was considered socially unacceptable. But, without invitation and taking a huge risk, this girl walks through the house, out to the courtyard, and into Jesus' presence. Indeed, into the presence of God!

Think about it: Cultural norms were telling her not to go into that room. Culture was telling her, "Play it safe—keep your distance. Don't risk getting close to Christ." But in her heart, something was compelling her to draw near to God. Something inside her longed for him, and she took the risk. She came to him. And Jesus met her, not with arms folded, but with arms wide open. That was the beginning of her unforgettable life.

You see, friend, maybe you don't go to church, and maybe you are not even sure why you are here today. But there is something in you that longs for God, that longs for your Creator. You long to be close to him and to have a relationship with him. The culture, however, and possibly even your friends are saying to you, "Keep your distance from Jesus. Don't risk it!" But if you just come to him, you'll be met with arms wide open. It will be the beginning of eternal life and an unforgettable life.

That is where it all starts. But, if you want to do something that will make your whole life unforgettable to God:

[II. Give God What You Cannot Keep Anyway]

"While Jesus was in Bethany in the home of a man known as Simon the Leper, a woman came to him with an alabaster jar of very expensive perfume."

Let's talk about this alabaster jar, because as we do, we get insight into the depths of this girl's love for Jesus. To begin with, this alabaster jar was not a jar. It was actually a flask made of carbonate of lime. These flasks were often rosebud shaped, and they were used to contain very expensive perfumes. This particular perfume was called *spikenard*, and John's gospel tells us that it was valued at three hundred denarii. You ask, "How much was that?" Converted to our currency, it would have been worth about twenty thousand dollars. In other words, this was high dollar perfume.

But you see, in those days, there were no banks where currency could be saved. So, people invested in valuable articles like this flask of perfume. It was a means of building financial security. Often a father would give such a vial of perfume to his daughter on the day she was born, and it would be the most precious thing she owned. So strong was its concentration, it was designed to last a lifetime.

But this dear girl comes into this courtyard—heart pounding, face flushed, and overwhelmed with love—and she pours the perfume on Jesus. "While Jesus was in Bethany in the home of a man known as Simon the Leper, a woman came to him with an alabaster jar of very expensive perfume, which she poured on his head as he was reclining at the table."

Now why did she do that? I mean, it does seem like overkill. But as you will see, it was not overkill. It was preparation for "after kill." Follow me, and I will explain: The timing of this act is only hours before Christ's arrest. Jesus will soon be arrested, tried, executed, and quickly buried. With that context in mind, let's pick up the rest of this narrative.

"When the disciples saw this, they were indignant. 'Why this waste?' they asked. 'This perfume could have been sold at a high price and the money given to the poor.' Aware of this, Jesus said to them, 'Why are you bothering this woman? She has done a beautiful thing to me ...When she poured this perfume on my body, she did it to prepare me for *burial*.'"

After Jesus left this house, the events that ushered in his execution began to unfold in rapid-fire sequence. In these days, when a person died, protocol was to quickly wrap the body in cloths and douse it with cheap perfume. This was to keep the body from stinking so badly. Jews did not embalm bodies, and so after death, the bodily stench would quickly get strong. To deal with this, they would immediately wrap it up in a mummy-like shroud and douse it in perfume until they could get the body in the tomb.

Somehow this young girl knew Jesus was going to die and be buried quickly. So she doused his body ahead of time—not with cheap perfume, but with the most expensive imaginable! Mind you, I don't think she took the time to overanalyze this: "Is this the right thing to do? Should I risk my financial security in a moment of overwhelming emotion?"

You see, God gives us the chance to give to something that will outlast our lives our money and our time. I think she just seized the chance to give to God. Think about it: If she had held onto her treasure, what would have been the effect? In the short term, it may have made life on earth easier—maybe. But she realized this was a once-in-a-lifetime chance to give to God. She was given an opportunity to give to God in a way that would be remembered forever. Ann Ortland, in her wonderful book called *Up with Worship*, writes:

"The delicious fragrance ran down over his shining hair and thick beard. It enfolded his body with its delightful aroma. Even his tunic and flowing undergarment were drenched with its enduring fragrance. Wherever he moved during the ensuing forty-eight hours, the perfume would go with him: into the upper room; into the garden of Gethsemane; into the High Priest's house; into Pilate's hall; and into the crude hands of those who cast lots for his clothing at the foot of the cross."

What a helpful insight! It reminds us that her devotion lingered with Jesus because, just hours after this, Jesus was arrested, tried, and crucified. And since his garments were never changed, the aroma went with him to his death. When everyone forsook him, when his friends betrayed him, when his enemies were ripping him to shreds, the fragrance reminded him! In fact, right up until his garments were removed and he was nailed to cross, the fragrance reminded him of this lady's love and devotion. And even then, the aroma remained on his hair.

What a beautiful reminder of how our gifts are not forgotten. Giving to God is one of the most unforgettable acts we can do for our Savior. On the way out today, you will be given a card with the perfume "Unforgettable" sprayed on it. It also has the outline of this sermon on it. Ladies, place it in your purse. Men, keep it in your wallet as a reminder of how to live an unforgettable life.

[III. Seize the Opportunity to Serve]
God gives us a once-in-a-lifetime opportunity to serve him. Sometimes those opportunities do not represent themselves. We can seize that chance and draw on the rewards for eternity, or we can forever lose the opportunity. Some of you just need to do something for God. You have thought about it and analyzed it, and the time and opportunities are fleeting by. You have a chance to do something for God that will be remembered forever.

It's amazing to me how many churches are unwilling to take a risk for God. They are so calculating that they have no concept of faith and risk. Their whole mantra is, "God, we played it safe with what you entrusted to us. God, we took the one talent you gave us and we buried it."

Multisensory Effect

The effect of the video made the message attracting, but the perfume on the card has almost immortalized this message. People tell me to this day that they carry the card in their wallet or purse. The scent reminds them and the outline reminds them of the path to living an unforgettable life.

SERMON 6: "CHILDREN UNDER CONSTRUCTION"

Level: Intermediate

Sermon Series: A Child

Sermon Title: Children under Construction

Sermon Text: Mark 10:13 – 16

Goal of Multisensory Illustration: To gain audience attention and create long-term memory.

Resources Needed

Materials: Concrete mix, wheelbarrow, shovels, construction work clothes, wood form shaped like a little child.

Technical Resources: None

Human Resources: Three to four people dressed in work clothes to help pour cement and to help spread it in the form.

Manuscript: As Spoken

I've got construction clothes on today, because I want to talk to you about a construction project. I want us to build something this coming year. I'm not talking about building an auditorium or a new gymnasium—nothing like that. I want you to help me build something far more important than any structure. I'm talking about building children. Specifically, building children for God. I want us to build children who are solid in their faith, children who are stable in what they believe, and children who can stand when their faith is challenged.

Now, to make a point about building solid children, I have premade the mold of a child, and I want some of you to help me build a child in this mold. Mind you, since we want to build a child who is solid and stable in the faith, we're going to build with cement. We're going to fill this child-like mold with wet cement. Come on up, folks. [*Helpers come on stage.*]

Think about it: Right now, the cement is wet, and that's a good thing, because we need to form it. Wet cement is moldable, pliable, and kind of teachable. I can easily work it. I can easily shape it to the mold. [*Pastor and helpers pour the wet cement into the child-shaped mold and spread it out with shovels so it conforms to the mold. The congregation watches the work.*]

But mark it: Once the cement starts to set, it is difficult to mold it. You have to mold it before it hardens. You have to shape it before it sets and becomes hard and impossible to work with.

Now, let me turn a corner and make a point: "Children are like wet cement." That phrase actually comes from a book written by Anne Ortland. You ask, "What do you mean?" Just this: Early on, the minds of children are pliable. Their faith can be shaped, and their beliefs can be molded to the Word of God. But as they get older, whatever they have come to believe—good or bad, true or false—starts to set like hardened cement. And if we are going to mold them by the Word of God, if we're going to shape them by the mold Jesus has given in the Word, we have to do it while "the cement is wet." We have to do it while they are young, before their hearts get hard.

Some research demonstrates that by age thirteen, most people's spiritual beliefs are irrevocably formed. In other words, what you believe by the time you are thirteen is what you will likely die believing. This doesn't discount life-changing experiences beyond this age, but these are the norms. Mark this down: Whoever shapes the child while the cement is wet is the one who molds the child. No one understood this more than Jesus.

Proposition: Jesus loves the little children. That's not just a cute song. It's also sound doctrine. Jesus cares about children. He wants to connect to them, and in this text he shows us how to connect children to him. He shows us how to build children with strong faith. Listen to me, Christ Fellowship: Jesus has called us to join him in building such children.

Interrogative: You ask, "How do we build children for Jesus?"

Transitional Statement: Let's find out as we look to the Bible.

[I. Jesus Loves the Little Children]

Let's sing that song together. [*Congregation sings song.*] Again, folks, that is not just a cutesy rhyme. That is the heartbeat of Jesus. Check it out in the narrative. "People were bringing *little children* to Jesus ... And he took the children *in his arms*, put his hands *on them* and *blessed them.*"

At this point in Jesus' ministry, wherever he went, massive crowds showed up to see him. Get the picture: For the past year and a half Jesus had been performing miracle after miracle, to the point that he has nearly banished disease from Palestine! He healed the sick, gave sight to the blind, and raised the dead, and it was incredible!

As we come to the scene of Mark 10, the crowds are electrified! So much so, that the disciples have to engage in crowd control to prevent Jesus from being mobbed. But watch what begins to happen: "People were bringing *little children* to Jesus to have him touch them." I love it! There was something about Jesus that made him approachable. There was something about Jesus that put people at ease. He created an environment that allowed people to get close to him, so much so that even little children were at ease with him.

Get it: Even though he was God Almighty in the flesh, little children were comfortable in his presence. Why? It is because Jesus loved the children, and they knew he loved them. He liked them, and they liked him. But mind you, there is another factor about Jesus and the children that fascinates me. Not only were the children attracted to him, but also, Jesus made time for them. "People were bringing little children to Jesus to have him touch them, but the disciples rebuked them."

Picture it: Mothers and fathers were trying to connect their children to Jesus, but the disciples were basically saying, "Get those kids out of here. Don't you know who this is? This is God Almighty in the flesh. He doesn't have time for children. He's too busy for kids." "When Jesus saw this, he was indignant." The word indignant is *aganakteo* in the Greek. To put it in the vernacular, it means "to be ticked off." When Jesus saw the disciples push the kids away from him, he was outraged. "When Jesus saw this, he was indignant. He said to them, 'Let the little children come to me.'" I love that!

Jesus carved out time to welcome children. He always took the time to invest in their lives and to build them up. Beyond that, Jesus knows Satan will make time for them. Satan has someone who will invest in them. Satan has someone who will shape their minds and hearts.

Jesus knew this fact: When children are young, their hearts are like wet cement. Their minds can be molded and shaped, and *someone* will mold them. The question is: Who? Who will mold the minds of children? The answer is, the one who invests time with them when they are wet cement.

Think of these facts: The average child spends twenty hours per week in front of the television listening and learning. The average parent talks to their child about thirty-eight minutes per week. Let me repeat the question: Who will shape the minds of our children? Answer: The one who invests time when they are wet cement!

Someone asked a top executive at MTV, "How does it feel to have the greatest influence on adolescents and teens?" The guy said: "We don't just have the greatest influence on them, we own them!" How could he make such a bold statement? The answer is simple: They spend time with the children when their minds are "wet cement."

Think of this: Children spend eight hours a day in public schools, and what do they traditionally hear? "You're not the unique creation of God. You have no accountability to God. You are a cosmological blunder of the universe." I love our teachers, but the public school system has made a formal commitment to indoctrinate children about life, and that wet cement is being warped into a mold that is anti-God and anti-Christ. Christians wonder why we are losing the battle for the minds of children. It's simple: Someone other than us is molding the cement while it's wet.

By the way: MTV spends an average of $1.4 million on a five-minute video. They have high-tech equipment and highly motivated people to sell explicit sexual music and scenes to our children. The average church, however, spends little or nothing on its children. We give our children's workers four white walls, a Fisher Price microphone, and say, "Go, win the kids." Then we try to convince the kids that we really care about them. Give me a break!

Make no mistake, Christ Fellowship: I am on a mission! I want our kids to have the best when it comes to teaching them about Jesus. I want to compete with Satan on a level with which he cannot compete. I want our children's ministry to have a state-of-the-art facility, high-tech equipment, devoted staff, and manpower from you. You may say, "I don't know how to teach kids. I don't know how to shape them." Let me give you an example of how to do it—from Jesus himself.

[II. Jesus' Model for Building Children]

"And he took the children in his arms, put his hands on them and [what?] blessed them." The word "blessed," *eulogeo*, means "to praise, to celebrate with praises, to give your blessing to someone." It's the idea that Jesus took the time to encourage these children. He spoke to them in a way that built them up. He spoke to them in a way that praised them. He got down on their level and reached out to them. "And he took the children in his arms."

What an example on how to do children's ministry! You don't have to be an expert. You don't have to be a rocket scientist. Let me give you the keys to reaching children for Jesus.

1. Jesus created an environment that made children **want** to be with him. Christ Fellowship, let's have a children's ministry that causes children to want to be here and to learn about Jesus. Some churches create an environment that makes children *not* to want to be with Jesus. The basic message sent to children by many churches is: "Jesus is *no fun*, and so there will be *no fun here*! Jesus is boring, and we intend to keep him that way."

More children have been bored away from Jesus than have ever been reasoned away from him. Our mission is to create a children's ministry that is as inviting and exciting as Jesus is himself—a children's ministry that is so exciting that kids are begging Mom and Dad, "Please, take me to church." We can create that, but only if you catch the vision and help.

2. Jesus **made time** for little children. Notice, I didn't say he *had* time for children. No, Jesus *made* time for them. He took the time to invest in their lives. This morning he's looking for some people who will give an hour each week to invest in the lives of children.

3. He spoke **words of encouragement** to them. "And he took the children in his arms, put his hands on them and *blessed* them." He blessed them with words of affirmation. "I love you. I care about you." And that is what we do in his place. We bless them with our own words. More than that, we tell them of Jesus' love and care for them. We teach them the truths of the Word. We shape their minds by his Word. In fact, the Word of God is the mold by which we build.

4. He **called** the children **to himself**. "When Jesus saw this, he was indignant. He said to them, 'Let the little children come to me.'" It really bothers me that some churches choose not to influence children with Jesus. Some churches and some parents adopt a "no influence policy" when it comes to Jesus and children—as if Jesus were not a Savior but some political or religious issue. They say something like this: "We choose not to influence our children about Jesus. We choose to let them find out for themselves. We choose to let them make up their own minds."

What a cop-out! Folks, do I have to remind you? This is not a political issue. This is not even a religious issue. This is a matter of eternal life and eternal death. Heaven and hell are at stake here. Granted, children have to make up their own minds at some point. God demands that. But if we don't teach them what to believe, someone else will teach them what to believe. Someone else will shape their minds into a mold that is not what God intends. Let me put it as simple as I know how: If we don't mold the cement while it's wet, Satan will have someone shape it into a mold that is anti-God and anti-Christ.

Look at this: The concrete is already starting to harden and set up. [*Pastor taps cement poured earlier with a shovel to demonstrate it is already beginning to harden.*] Here's the kind of workers we need:

- Teachers: To put in the concrete. The Bible gives us the mold.
- Blessers: People who can build children by just being in the class, listening to them, and encouraging them.
- Construction workers: To make sure the teacher has all he or she needs to teach.
- Givers: We need to finance the work.

And listen, when you come to work with the kids, don't come in formal attire. Come in casual work clothes. There is work to be done.

Multisensory Effect

The effect of this message was unforgettable. Many people volunteered to work with our kids as a result of this message.

EPILOGUE

YOU HAVE TO READ THIS STORY

WRITING WITH TEARS IN MY EYES

I am writing this on Christmas Eve night just following our 2007 Christmas Eve service, and tears are welling up in my eyes as I type. Mind you, my manuscript for *The Power of Multisensory Preaching and Teaching* has already gone to the publisher, but I hope they allow me to add this story. Here's what happened.

Tonight, Pastor Eric Geiger spoke during our Christmas Eve service. I decided to sit in the rear of the auditorium so I could experience a Christmas worship service for the first time in many years. There are many experiences we pastors miss, simply because we are busy speaking while the Holy Spirit is working in the audience. This was one experience, however, I was destined to see. Follow the events.

As the music portion of the worship drew to a conclusion, a young couple came in and sat at the rear of the auditorium. They were just in front and to the left of where I was seated. With them were their two little boys, both of whom took their seats between the wife and husband. Within minutes, a life-and-death struggle began to unfold before me … an *eternal life* and *eternal death* struggle.

Eric began to teach from Luke 19:10, "For the Son of Man came to seek and to save what was lost." The message was a powerful unpacking of the Christmas rescue mission. As he taught, however, I noticed this husband never looked up to make eye contact with Eric. In fact, he appeared hell-bent on *not* looking up. He looked down, instead, at his wallet and busied himself by shuffling his credit cards and money. At the same time this was going on, I could tell his wife was a believer. It was clear that she had invited him to the service in hopes that he would meet the Savior.

As Eric spoke the wonderful message of rescue, the wife continually reached her hand across the two little boys over to her husband's shoulder. Lovingly and pleadingly she admonished him to look up, but he refused. Interestingly, I could tell he loved his wife, but it was clear he didn't want to be in church. Perhaps, he came only to humor her or to get her off his case. At any rate, twenty minutes went by, and the young husband continued to bury his face in his wallet. By now, his wife looked as if she was dying within. It was clear he was not going to connect to the message or to Christ.

Then, however, Eric began to make a point about a certain United States Marine, Dave Karnes, whose bravery and rescue mission was documented in the Oliver Stone movie *World Trade Center*. After briefly describing the true event, Eric had the media team launch a series of video clips from the movie.

HE LOOKED UP!

Folks, as soon as that clip came on the screen, this young husband looked up! I couldn't believe my eyes! It was the first time he had paid attention in the entire message. I watched him like a hawk, and I prayed for his soul. Here is the story behind the film clips, and this is the drama he witnessed as the film rolled.

Dave Karnes, an ex-Marine turned businessman, saw the World Trade Center events unfolding on television just like the rest of us did. As he watched, however, he felt compelled to go down to New York City to help out. The film clip shows the moving words of President Bush telling the nation that we are under attack. As the President spoke, the former Marine said, "I have to go down there to help."

From there, the film chronicled the response of Karnes as he prepared for his mission. First, he went to church to pray. Next, he went to the barber and had his head shaved Marine-style. Finally, after putting on his military garb, he got in his Porsche and drove 120 mph down to lower Manhattan. By the way, I checked the attention of the audience at Christ Fellowship — *every* eye was riveted to the screens.

The next clip moved seamlessly to the wreckage of the World Trade Center. The ex-Marine was allowed to go inside the rubble of the buildings. The film follows the Marine as he shines his flashlight in the darkness and calls out to any survivors. Suddenly he hears a trapped man call out in the darkness. The man was Will Jimeno, who along with John McLaughlin had survived the tragedy.

Jimeno screams out to the Marine, "Please, don't leave us! Please, don't leave us!" The Marine then said something I'll never forget as long as I live: "Sir, we are the United States Marines. *You are our mission!*"

The young husband in front of me never took his eyes off the screens. He was locked in. Then, Eric began to draw the connection between the rescue mission of that Marine and the rescue mission of Christ. He said this: "If you are here tonight and you have never trusted Christ, you need to know that you are in danger of being lost forever. You are in danger of being separated from God forever. Christ came for the express purpose of rescuing you. *You are his mission.*"

At that exact moment, the husband reached over to his wife and touched her on the hand, signaling that he was under conviction. His wife's eyes filled with tears and so did mine. Eric then called for a commitment, and I watched as this man prayed to receive the Lord. Later he filled out a communication card.

Then, at the conclusion of the service, I saw one more thing that blew me away. To close out the service, our congregation sang the song "Rescue." Almost everyone raised his or her hands in praise to God. This young man, who had just trusted Christ, slowly raised his hands and tried to sing the song with us. I felt like a silent observer to the rescuing work of the Holy Spirit.

But don't miss the point: The man was totally disconnected until that visual video was introduced. The Holy Spirit used that clip to draw that man to Christ. Mind you, Eric is a phenomenal communicator in his own right. But it took a visual aid to grab this man's attention. I suppose it will be easy to criticize what I saw, but think of this: If this man were your friend or your child or your husband or your wife, would you be so critical? Or would you praise God for Eric's passion to do whatever it takes to connect to the unsaved of our world?

My prayer is that you will witness this kind of effect as you use multisensory teaching. My prayer for you is that you will have similar stories that change the lives and destinations of people forever.

APPENDIX
A

RESEARCH DESIGN AND METHODOLOGY

RESEARCH PURPOSE

In light of Bible teaching objectives, the goal of this research was to explore the relationship between three preaching methodologies and student *attention, comprehension,* and *retention.* Those different teaching methods are:

1. Monosensory teaching: Verbal Communication
2. Multisensory teaching: Verbal + Visual Communication
3. Advanced multisensory teaching: Verbal + Visual + Interactive Communication

DESIGN OVERVIEW

Under the direction of doctoral advisors at Southern Baptist Theological Seminary, three separate weekend experiments were conducted to determine the relationship of the three different teaching methodologies to student attention, comprehension, and retention of teaching material.

The experiments consisted of three Quasi-Experimental Post-test Only Control Group Designs. The design is patterned after the model given in the textbook *Practical Research: Planning and Design,* by Paul Leedy and Jeanne Ormord.[1] The only difference is that we would be working with a much larger sample than the one used in the book.

The independent variable was the different teaching methodologies and the dependent variable was the effect on attention, comprehension, and retention. Post-test data was subsequently gathered to measure influence. The sample was stratified into three groupings from the three services:

1. *Control Sample* — Tx: Exposure to monosensory delivery
2. *Test Sample 1* — Tx^1: Exposure to multisensory delivery.
3. *Test Sample 2* — Tx^2: Exposure to advanced multisensory delivery.

The experiments unfolded in the following sequence:

Week 1: The researcher developed an expository sermon, which was delivered three times.

1. The first delivery was to the *Saturday evening* congregation, and the delivery style was *verbal, visual, and interactive.*
2. The second delivery of the identical sermon was to the *Sunday A-hour* congregation, and the delivery style was *verbal.*
3. The final delivery of the identical sermon was to the *Sunday B-hour* congregation, and the delivery style was *verbal and visual.*

Week 2: The researcher developed a second expository, which was delivered three times.

1. The first delivery was to the *Saturday evening* congregation, and the delivery style was *verbal.*
2. The second delivery of the identical sermon was to the *Sunday A-hour* congregation, and the delivery style was *verbal and visual.*
3. The final delivery of the identical sermon was to the *Sunday B-hour* congregation, and the delivery style was *verbal, visual, and interactive.*

Week 3: The researcher developed a third expository message, which was delivered three times.

1. The first delivery was to the *Saturday evening* congregation, and the delivery style was *verbal and visual.*
2. The second delivery of the identical sermon was to the *Sunday A-hour* congregation, and the delivery style was *verbal, visual, and interactive.*
3. The final delivery of the identical sermon was to the *Sunday B-hour* congregation, and the delivery style was *verbal.*

POPULATION SAMPLE

The experiment was conducted at the Christ Fellowship in Miami, Florida. The population provided several advantages for conducting such an experiment:

1. The context afforded the researcher a diverse population with a membership comprised of sixty-one nationalities. Statistics are based on church records as of April 2004.
2. The geographical context in which the church is located demonstrates a broad range of educational and socioeconomic diversity.[2]

3. The church provided three separate services in which to conduct the three-pronged Quasi-Experimental test.

4. A total of 1,604 adults participated in the testing. All of those who met the criteria for the testing were evaluated, and those who did not meet the criteria were eliminated from the test results. In the end, a total of 923 samples were considered viable test samples.

TAKING ATTENTION MEASUREMENTS

Audience attention was measured by observing a sample of individuals from each service during the monosensory and multisensory deliveries. Observation was accomplished by use of high-resolution camera viewing and video recordings. Post-treatment observations from the videotapes marked the number of audience distractions during the monosensory deliveries and during the multisensory deliveries. Data was subsequently gathered to determine the relationship of the teaching methodologies to audience attention.

Precedent literature confirmed that *basic* attention could be measured through retention tests subsequent to teaching exposure. Measuring *levels* of attention, however, requires observation. These include retention observations, eye fixations, and viewing times.[3]

During treatment observations. Following this precedent, this researcher sought to measure attention levels by the observation of individuals who sat in a specified area of the auditorium during the presentation of each teaching methodology. Cameras were focused on those individuals during presentation of teaching methods. This sample was smaller than the comprehension and retention samples, because cameras had to be able to focus on the eyes of each individual.

Levels of attention were measured by observation of eye fixations and viewing times. "Observational measures of attention require that a classroom rater make some judgment regarding the focus of student attention."

Observational procedures often require that the rater judge which of the several categories of behavior best describe a student's actions during a brief interval of time. A behavioral definition of attentiveness — inattentiveness within such a system may include a list of specific activities (orients eyes to text or teacher, observes chalkboard, closes eyes, works or plays with nonassigned materials, etc.) or a general description of focus (e.g., pupil is doing what is appropriate in the situation).[4]

Post-treatment observations. After filming, a panel of "classroom raters" viewed the films and focused on each individual during the specified time and then plotted scores for them. The scores were determined by the number of head movements and eye distractions away from the determined point of focus. The panel was instructed not to count head and eye movements such as taking notes or laughing as distractions. The individuals were anonymous and designated by a number, not their names.

TAKING COMPREHENSION AND RETENTION MEASUREMENTS

Audience comprehension and retention were measured by a fill-in-the-blank test given at the conclusion of the final week of treatment. Questions were designed to determine student comprehension and retention of material taught during the monosensory treatments, multisensory treatments, and advanced multisensory treatments.

In order to participate in the test, the individuals had to meet the two following criteria:

1. Be present for all three weeks of the testing, so that they were treated with all three teaching methods.
2. Answer all questions on the test.

Data was subsequently gathered to determine the relationship of the teaching methodologies to student comprehension and retention. In all tests, the independent variable was the teaching methodology and the dependent variables were attention, comprehension, and retention. The experiment unfolded over three weekends of teaching.

At the conclusion of the post test, data was gathered to determine the relationship of the teaching methodologies to student comprehension and retention. Cross tabulations with Chi-squared tests were conducted to test for differences in the percentage of subjects who answered correctly by type of delivery. These tests were carried out on the retention and comprehension items for each week separately since the survey was administered only once. For significant Chi-squared tests, post hoc pair-wise comparisons of types of delivery were performed using Holm's sequential Bonferroni procedure to control for the probability of Type I error. All tests were significant if < .05. SPSS for Windows (v.12) was used for all tests.

CONTROLLING CONFOUNDING VARIABLES

1. The teacher was the same in all three treatments.
2. The message was the same in all three treatments.

3. The context was the same in all three treatments.
4. The samples were selected randomly and voluntarily.
5. A cross section of race, age, and culture was achieved.
6. Even though the groups were selected randomly, education, motivation, and other variables were uncontrollable. The random selection should have given a proper mix of these variables.
7. Each participant remained anonymous.
8. Each group was given the same post-test.
9. The Hawthorne Effect was controlled, as the samples were unaware of the experiment until the time of the post-test.
10. The researcher recognizes he could deliberately influence the outcomes of the tests by not being enthusiastic about the lecture sermon. Therefore, an individual was recruited to observe this pastor-researcher as he delivered the nine sermons to the congregation. The individual had this to say: "The pastor-researcher was extremely passionate about all sermon deliveries and did not appear to alter his delivery other than the type of methodology."

APPENDIX B

SERMON SERIES USING ARTWORK

SERIES CONTENT

This was one of the most moving sermon series I have ever conducted. A total of six messages focused on six attributes of God. The first message described God's mercy, and it was preceded by worship about mercy and a painting of God's hand reaching down. The second message was about judgment and the painting depicted God's hand reaching upward. The third was on compassion, and the painting before that message portrayed God's heart. The fourth message was on God's jealousy, and the painting depicted God's throne. The fifth message was on God's wisdom, and the art portrayed God's head. The final message was on holiness, depicted by God's feet. The following shows the paintings of each attribute and how they were rendered during the messages:

1. Mercy: God's hand reaching down

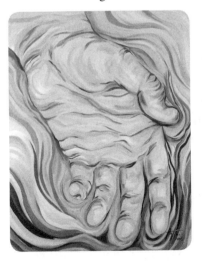

2. Judgment: God's hand reaching up

3. Compassion: God's heart

4. Jealousy: God's throne

5. Wisdom: God's head

6. Holiness: God's feet

During the final message on holiness, four of the paintings were suspended vertically from the ceiling of the worship center. The head of God was at the top, then in descending order came the heart, the throne, and the feet. The idea was to depict the vertical cross member.

Focusing on God's holiness, the question of the final message was this: How can sinful people ever come into the presence of such a holy God? At the end of the message we gave the answer in picture form. I placed red paint in the middle of God's feet, indicating the piercing of his feet on the cross. Next, I placed red paint on each of the hands that had been painted and were now resting off to each side of the stage.

Then, the hands of God were raised by a group from our drama crew into the position of crucifixion. As they were raised, our worship band led the congregation to sing, "When I Survey the Wondrous Cross." There were few dry eyes in the congregation.

POWER SOURCE + POWER LINES = POWER RECEIVED

I am writing the conclusion to this section by candlelight, because we just lost power to our house. I called Florida Power and Light on my cell phone and they told me that there is a power outage in our area affecting 809 homes.

Mind you, the problem is not with the nuclear power plant. Talk about power! The Turkey Point Nuclear Power Plant in Miami generates about 1,400 million watts of electricity — enough power to supply the annual needs of more than 450,000 homes. So, the problem is not a power source issue.

The problem is not with our house either. Our home is wired to receive the energy that the Turkey Point nuclear reactor transmits to us. Nevertheless, Rhonda and I are sitting at the counter in the dimly lit kitchen. She is reading a novel by candlelight and I am scribbling this point as best I can with only the light of the candle.

The question still remains: Why are we not receiving power? The reason is quite simple. There is a power *line* down between the nuclear power plant and us. The weakness is not in the power source, and the weakness is not in the capacity of our house to receive the power. The weakness is in the power lines that *transmit* the power.

What a picture of preaching. We have a literal powerhouse in the Word of God. "The Word of God is living and active," says Hebrews 4:12. The Bible has unbelievable amounts of power, because it carries the power of God himself.

On the receiving ends, people are wired by God to receive that Word. Those of us who are saved have the Holy Spirit to receive that Word and to connect it to our lives. Even the lost have the ability to receive that power of God's Word and thereby be saved.

When you add it up, the breakdown is not in the power plant of the Word, and it is not in the receiving side of human beings. The breakdown is most often in the communication line between the Word and the audience, that is, in the teacher. We are often boring, unclear, and very forgettable. When that happens, our audience is left "sitting in the dark."

Multisensory communication has a way of making sure that that breakdown never happens. Multisensory communication transmits our message to multiple sensory receptors and increases audience attention, comprehension, and retention levels.

ENDNOTES

PART 1: Presenting the Multisensory Effect

1. Jim Collins, *Good to Great: Why Some Companies Make the Leap and Others Don't* (New York: Harper Business, 2001), 1.

CHAPTER 1 — Welcome: To the Multisensory Revolution

1. John MacArthur, *Why Government Can't Save You: An Alternative to Political Activism* (Nashville, TN: Nelson, 2000), 69.

2. Michael Parkinson, "Billion Dollar Graphics: 3 Easy Steps to Turn Your Ideas into Persuasive Visuals and Billion Dollar Graphics: 40 Powerful Ways to Show Your Ideas," publication available from 3M Corporation.

3. Lynell Burmark, *Visual Literacy: Learn to See, See to Learn* (Alexandria, VA: Vision Shift International, 2006).

4. Roy B. Zuck, *Teaching As Jesus Taught* (Grand Rapids: Baker, 1995), 89.

5. Parkinson, "Billion Dollar Graphics."

6. Maurice Francis Kalin, "The Influence of Choice on the Acquisition and Retention of Learning Materials in Different Modes of Instruction" (EdD diss., West Virginia University, 1972), 6.

7. Stephen Brookfield, *Becoming a Critically Reflective Teacher* (San Francisco: Jossey-Bass, 1995), 29.

8. Collins, *Good to Great*, 3.

CHAPTER 2 — Elevate: From Good to Phenomenal Communication

1. Haddon Robinson and Torrey Robinson, *It's All in How You Tell It: Preaching First-Person Expository Messages* (Grand Rapids: Baker, 2003), 9.

2. Ibid., 9.

3. Henri J. Nouwen, *Creative Ministry* (New York: Doubleday, 1978), 23.

4. James D. Berkley, ed., *Leadership Handbook of Preaching and Worship: Practical Insight from a Cross Section of Ministry Leaders* (Grand Rapids: Baker, 1992), 93.

5. Reg Grant and John Reed, *The Power Sermon: Countdown to Quality Messages for Maximum Impact* (Grand Rapids: Baker, 1993), 11.

6. David J. Hesselgrave, *Communicating Christ Cross-Culturally: An Introduction to Missionary Communication* (Grand Rapids: Zondervan, 1991), 537 (emphasis in original).

7. Christakis A. Dimitiri, Frederick J. Zimmerman, David L. Digiuseppe, and Carolyn A. McCarty, "Early Television Exposure and Subsequent Attentional Problems in Children," *Pediatrics* 113/4 (2004): 8 – 9.

8. John R. W. Stott, *Between Two Worlds: The Art of Preaching in the Twentieth Century* (Grand Rapids: Eerdmans, 1982), 70.

CHAPTER 3 — Expect: Dramatic Results

1. Tony Evans, *Called for a Purpose* (Dallas, TX: Urban Alternative, 2005), cassette.

2. Walter C. Kaiser Jr., *Toward an Exegetical Theology* (Grand Rapids: Baker, 1981), 81.

3. Joseph M. Stowell III, "Preaching for Change," in *The Big Idea of Biblical Preaching: Connecting the Bible to People*, ed. Keith Willhite and Scott M. Gibson (Grand Rapids: Baker, 1998), 125.

4. See Benjamin S. Bloom, *Taxonomy of Educational Objectives: Handbook 1* (New York: David McKay, 1956).

5. Paul D. Leedy and Jeanne E. Ormord, *Practical Research: Planning and Design*, 7th ed. (Upper Saddle River, NJ: Prentice-Hall, 2003), 237.

6. Gary D. Phye and Thomas Andre, eds., *Cognitive Classroom Learning: Understanding, Thinking and Problem Solving* (New York: Academic Press, 1986), 58.

7. Robinson and Robinson, *It's All in How You Tell It*, 9 – 10.

8. H. Hanse, *"echo," Theological Dictionary of the New Testament*, ed. G. Kittel; trans. G. W. Bromiley (Grand Rapids: Eerdmans, 1964 –), 2:816.

9. B. Reicke, *"pros," Theological Dictionary of the New Testament*, 6:720.

10. See the standard New Testament Greek dictionary, *A Greek-English Lexicon of the New Testament*, ed. Walter Bauer, Frederick W. Danker, et al., 3rd ed. (Chicago: Univ. of Chicago Press, 2000) (abbreviated BDAG), under *prosecho*, meaning 2, p. 880.

11. J. Behm, *"katanoeo," Theological Dictionary of the New Testament*, 4:974 – 95.

12. Roy B. Zuck, *Teaching as Paul Taught* (Grand Rapids: Baker, 1998), 159 (italics added).

13. See BDAG, under *suniemi*, p. 972.

14. This study was published in *The International Journal of Science* (May 28, 1999), 1531 – 33. See also Brenda Melo, Gordan Winocur, and Morris Moscovitch, "False Recall and False Recognition: An Examination of the Effects of Selective and Combined Lesions to the Medial Temporal Lobe/Diencephalons and Frontal Lobe Structures," *Psychology Press* (1999), 343 – 44.

15. Tony I. Rushworth and R. E. Passingham, "Specialization within the Prefrontal Cortex: The Ventral Prefrontal Cortex and Associative Learning" (2000),

103 – 13. Retrieved 2 March 2003 from www.ncbi.nih.gov/query.fcgi?cmd=Retri eve&db=PubMed&list.

CHAPTER 4 — Eyewitness: The Neurological Proof

1. Linda Verlee Williams, *A Guide to Right Brain/Left Brain Education: Teaching for the Two-Sided Mind* (New York: Simon & Schuster, 1983), 114.

2. Walter B. Barbee and Raymond H. Swassing, *Teaching Modality Strengths: Concepts and Practices* (Columbus, OH: Zaner-Bloser, 1979), 1.

3. Phye and Andre, eds., *Cognitive Classroom Learning*, 51.

4. Samuel Bogoch, *The Biochemistry of Memory: With an Inquiry into the Function of Brain Mucoids* (New York: Oxford Univ. Press, 1968), 47.

5. Ibid., 39 (italics added).

6. Richard S. Lazarus, ed., *Sensory Psychology* (Englewood Cliffs, NJ: Prentice-Hall, 1965), 3.

7. Lynn Hamilton, *Facing Autism: Giving Parents Reasons for Hope and Guidance for Help* (Colorado Springs, CO: Waterbrook, 2000), 210.

8. A. T. Robertson, *Word Pictures in the New Testament* (Nashville, TN: Broadman, 1932), 5:205.

9. G. Delling, *"aistheterion,"* *Theological Dictionary of the New Testament*, 1:187.

10. Ibid., 1:188. Recall here too what was said in ch. 3 about *katanoeo* in Heb. 3:1. Even the Scriptures recognize the link between the senses and the brain in the learning process.

11. See Mariaemma Willis and Victoria Kindle Hodson, *Discover Your Child's Learning Style: Children Learn in Unique Ways — Here's the Key to Every Child's Learning Success* (Rocklin, CA: Prima, 1999), 145.

12. Lazarus, *Sensory Psychology*, 7 (italics added).

13. As noted in Thomas Armstrong, *Multiple Intelligences in the Classroom* (Alexandria, VA: Association for Supervision and Curriculum Development, 1994), 54 (italics added).

14. Colin Blakemore, *Mechanics of the Mind* (New York: Cambridge Univ. Press, 1977), 86 – 87 (italics added).

15. Robert Ulrich, *Education in Western Culture* (New York: Harcourt, Brace and World, 1965), 93.

16. Tom Schultz and Joani Schultz, *Why Nobody Learns Much of Anything at Church and How to Fix It* (Loveland, CO: Group, 1993), 106.

17. As noted in Willis and Hodson, *Discover Your Child's Learning Style*, 155.

18. Ibid.

19. John MacArthur, *Why Government Can't Save You: An Alternative to Political Activism* (Nashville, TN: Nelson, 2000), 69 (italics added).

20. *The Journal of the American Medical Association* lists several archived studies, which discuss brain hemisphere distinctions; see "A Function of Magnetic Resonance Imaging Study of Left Hemisphere Dominance in Children," *JAMA & Archives* 59 (2002): 13 – 18.

21. Fergus Reilly, "Eyesight: Brain Hemisphere Utilization," 3 – 4, retrieved 8 October 2003 from www.cybersayer.com/eyesite/hemsphr.html.

22. See David A. Sousa, *How the Brain Learns: A Classroom Teacher's Guide* (Thousand Oaks, CA: Corwin, 2001), 31.

23. Findley B. Edge, *Teaching for Results* (Nashville, TN: Broadman & Holman, 1956), 42.

24. See Barbee and Swassing, *Teaching Modality Strengths*, vii.

25. William R. Yount, *Created to Learn: A Christian Teacher's Introduction to Educational Psychology* (Nashville, TN: Broadman & Holman, 1996), 240.

26. G. Pask, "Techniques in the Study and Practice of Education," *British Journal of Educational Psychology* 46 (1976): 13 – 25.

27. See, for example, Fredrick G. Morton, "An Explanatory Study of the Relationship between the Multiple Intelligences and the Preferred Teaching Method of Select Youth Ministers" (PhD diss., New Orleans Baptist Theological Seminary, 1999), 26.

28. MacArthur, *Why Government Can't Save You*, 69 (italics added).

29. Barbee and Swassing, *Teaching Modality Strengths*, 14.

30. Morton, "An Explanatory Study," 108.

31. Robert W. Pazmiño, *Principles and Practices of Christian Education* (Grand Rapids: Baker, 2002), 108.

32. Harvey Silver and J. Robert Hanson, *Learning Styles and Strategies* (Woodbridge, NJ: Thoughtful Education Press, 1996).

CHAPTER 5 — Embrace: The Theological Endorsement

1. Arthur W. Hunt, *The Vanishing Word: The Veneration of Visual Imagery in the Postmodern World* (Wheaton, IL: Crossway, 2003), 190.

2. Bryon Snapp, "The Vanishing Word: The Veneration of Visual Imagery," retrieved March 2004 from PCANews.com (see www.christianity.com/CC/CDA/CC_Home/CC_Search_ts/1,PTID23682|C.

3. John MacArthur, *Ashamed of the Gospel: When the Church Becomes Like the World* (Wheaton, IL: Crossway, 1993), 69.

4. Andy Stanley and Ed Young, *Can We Do That? Innovative Practices That Will Change the Way You Do Church* (West Monroe, LA: Howard, 2002), 155.

5. See www.edwinhubble.com/hubble_quotes.htm (retrieved February 2008).

6. Calvin Miller, *The Empowered Communicator: Seven Keys to Unlocking an Audience* (Nashville, TN: Broadman & Holman, 1994), 15 – 16.

7. Zuck, *Teaching As Paul Taught*, 178.

8. MacArthur, *Ashamed of the Gospel*, 69.

9. Ibid., 69–70.

10. Miller, *The Empowered Communicator*, 152–53.

CHAPTER 6 — Experience: The Power of Bible Exposition and Multisensory Communication

1. www.fastcompany.com/magazine/06/writestuff.html (retrieved February 2008).

2. Kaiser, *Toward an Exegetical Theology*, 7–8.

3. As cited in ibid., 7.

4. John MacArthur, *Rediscovering Expository Preaching* (Dallas: Word, 1992), 22–23.

5. Dan Kimball, as spoken at Arts Conference, Willow Creek Association, Barrington, IL.

6. Thom S. Rainer, *Surprising Insights from the Unchurched* (Grand Rapids: Zondervan, 2001), 45.

PART 2: Preparing a Multisensory Message

1. Collins, *Good to Great*, 3.

CHAPTER 8 — Process: Designing Multisensory Journeys

1. This was a word that was developed by the team as a word that works, even though its meaning may not have the most positive connotations.

CHAPTER 9 — Procedures: Effective Use of Multisensory Components

1. John F. MacArthur, *The Glory of Heaven: The Truth about Heaven, Angels, and Eternal Life* (Wheaton, IL: Crossway, 1996), 85.

2. Max Lucado, *Cure for the Common Life: Living in Your Sweet Spot* (Nashville, TN: W Publishing Group, 2005), 51–52.

3. Andy Stanley, *Intimacy with God* (DVD; Alpharetta, GA: North Point Ministries Inc.).

CHAPTER 10 — Attention: Make Sure *You* Get It

1. This is a view held by many of the Catholic people in Miami. Again, most of the Miami population is non-Protestant.

2. See BDAG, under *elenchos*, p. 315.

CHAPTER 11 — Comprehension: Make Sure *They* Get It

1. Bill Hybels, "The Power of Clarity" (Barrington, IL: Willow Creek Association, 2006), CDLS0610.

2. W. Grundmann, *"eusemos,"* *Theological Dictionary of the New Testament*, 2:770.

3. *The Passion of the Christ* is a movie with many violent parts (for which reason it has been rated R); if there are children in your audience, it is not recommended that these parts be shown.

4. George Wald, "Life: How Did It Get Here?" *Scientific American* (August 1954), 46.

APPENDIX A — Research Design and Methodology

1. Leedy and Ormord, *Practical Research*.

2. Leavall Center for Evangelism and Church Growth, *A Demographic Study of Miami, Florida (5 Mile Ring) for FBC Perrine* (New Orleans: New Orleans Baptist Theological Seminary, 2002), 4.

3. Phye and Andre, eds., *Cognitive Classroom Learning*, 58.

4. Ibid., 59.

PHOTO CREDITS

Share Your Thoughts

With the Author: Your comments will be forwarded to the author when you send them to *zauthor@zondervan.com*.

With Zondervan: Submit your review of this book by writing to *zreview@zondervan.com*.

Free Online Resources at

www.zondervan.com/hello

 Zondervan AuthorTracker: Be notified whenever your favorite authors publish new books, go on tour, or post an update about what's happening in their lives.

 Daily Bible Verses and Devotions: Enrich your life with daily Bible verses or devotions that help you start every morning focused on God.

 Free Email Publications: Sign up for newsletters on fiction, Christian living, church ministry, parenting, and more.

 Zondervan Bible Search: Find and compare Bible passages in a variety of translations at www.zondervanbiblesearch.com.

 Other Benefits: Register yourself to receive online benefits like coupons and special offers, or to participate in research.